Teacher's Classroom Manual

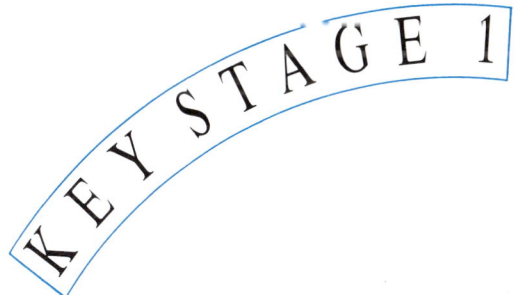

Stephen Hopkins

Anne Hunter

(Bishop Grosseteste College)

Nelson

Thomas Nelson and Sons Ltd
Nelson House Mayfield Road
Walton-on-Thames Surrey
KT12 5PL UK

51 York Place
Edinburgh
EH1 3JD UK

Thomas Nelson (Hong Kong) Ltd
Toppan Building 10/F
22A Westlands Road
Quarry Bay Hong Kong

Thomas Nelson Australia
480 La Trobe Street
Melbourne Victoria 3000
Australia

Nelson Canada
1120 Birchmount Road
Scarborough Ontario
M1K 5G4 Canada

© Bishop Grosseteste College 1990

First published by Thomas Nelson and Sons Ltd in co-operation with Bishop Grosseteste College, Lincoln, 1990

ISBN 0-17-423184-9

NPN 9 8 7 6 5 4 3 2 1

All rights reserved. This publication is protected in the United Kingdom by the Copyright, Design and Patents Act 1988 and in other countries by comparable legislation.

The publisher grants permission for copies of figures 3, 4 and 5, the evaluation checklists in section 3, and the tables of science opportunities in play activities in section 4 to be made without fee as follows:

Private purchasers may make copies for their own use or for use by their own students; school purchasers may make copies for use within and by the staff and students of the school only. This permission to copy does not extend to additional schools or branches of an institution, who should purchase a separate master copy of the book for their own use.

For copying in any other circumstances prior permission in writing must be obtained from Thomas Nelson and Sons Ltd.

Printed in Hong Kong.

The authors and publishers are grateful to the following for their help:

All Saints C of E Primary School
North Hykeham
Lincoln

Mount Street County Infant School
Lincoln

St Mary's C of E Primary School
Welton
Lincolnshire

St Faiths C of E
School, Lincoln

Long Bennington C of E Primary School
Long Bennington
Lincolnshire

Nettleham County Infants
School, Nettleham, Lincoln

St Stephens School,
London SW 8

Bishop Grosseteste College
Lincoln

The extracts from *Science in the National Curriculum* are reproduced with the permission of the Controller of Her Majesty's Stationery Office.

The extract by Margaret Tait from the *International Journal of Early Childhood* is reproduced with the permission of the Ontario Institute for Studies in Education, Toronto.

All photographs by Chris Ridgers except those from the following sources:
Bruce Coleman, pp. 83 (top left), 89, 90 (all), 96 (bottom), 103 (bottom), 119 (bottom), 120 (both left), Richard & Sally Greenhill, 134, The Image Bank, 96 (top left), 126 (both), The Image Bank/Stockphotos, 96 (top), p.135 (bottom) by John Urling-Clark.

Cover illustration by Tom Saecker.

Contents

Introduction iv

Section 1 Planning Science
Planning and record keeping for key stage 1 1
Using the themes and units 3

Section 2 Organising Science in the Infant Classroom
Thinking about organisation 13
A framework for teaching and learning 14
Evaluation 19

Section 3 Science Units
How to use this section 21

Light
Unit 1 Light, shadows, colours and mirrors 22

Sounds
Unit 2 Sounds 30

Batteries, buzzers and bulbs
Unit 3 How to make bulbs light and buzzers sound 38

How people change the environment
Unit 4 Improving the appearance of the local environment 46

Themselves and others and how to keep healthy
Unit 5 Growing and moving 54
Unit 6 Using the senses 62
Unit 7 Feeding 70

Plants
Unit 8 How to take care of plants 78
Unit 9 How plant life varies 86
Unit 10 Seasonal and daily changes in plants 92

Animals
Unit 11 How to take care of animals 98
Unit 12 How animal life varies 106
Unit 13 Seasonal and daily changes in animals 114

Sky and weather
Unit 14 Changes in the weather and the effect of the weather 122
Unit 15 Changes in the sky: light and dark 130
Unit 16 Changes in temperature: hot and cold 138

Moving things
Unit 17 How to make things move 146

Materials
Unit 18 Natural materials found in the locality: stones, rocks, soil 154
Unit 19 Everyday substances which melt and solidify: ice/water, wax, chocolate etc. 162
Unit 20 Everyday materials: sand, wood, metal, plastics, paper, clay, fabrics (including magnets) 170
Unit 21 Using materials to make structures 178
Evaluation checklist for IT 184

Section 4 Science in Play Activities 185
The sand tray 187
The water tray 190
Toys 194
Role play 197
Modelling with everyday materials 201

Introduction

The purpose of this manual is to provide support for the teacher in planning and implementing science in the curriculum of 5-7 year olds.

Section 1 gives the teacher and the school guidance on planning science in the context of an integrated infant curriculum. The scheme outlined here will ensure that children experience a balanced and progressive coverage of the **National Curriculum** in science and that scientific learning experiences can be provided for children as part of a cross-curricular approach.

Section 2 gives a general framework for teaching and learning science in the infant classroom. The framework has been devised to help the teacher plan, organise, manage and evaluate science learning opportunities in a wide range of classroom settings. It would be valuable to read this general section before the particular guidance and support for each of the units which make up section 3.

Section 3 comprises 21 units, each of which starts with a list of the learning opportunities which the unit's knowledge and understanding content could provide. In each unit the relationship between these learning opportunities and the National Curriculum **programme of study** and **attainment target levels** is clearly demonstrated. **Assessment and evaluation** are also addressed. The guidance and suggestions in each of the 21 units are structured on the framework for teaching and learning outlined in section 2.

Section 4 provides guidance for teachers in exploiting the scientific learning potential of play activities. These can be a rich context for the development of scientific skills, concepts and attitudes.

The Nelson Science materials

Science Explorers

Three booklets, forming **Science Explorers**, support children's scientific exploration and investigation in key stage 1. The three booklets are colour coded to correspond to the three forms of question used in this manual:
- **I wonder whether . . . (Carrying Out Surveys 1)**
- **What happens if . . . (Experimenting 1)**
- **Can we find a way to . . . (Problem Solving 1)**

There is an annotated version of each booklet for the teacher in the **Teacher's Guide to Science Explorers 1**.

Picture Resource Books

These provide the teacher with a range of carefully selected pictorial resource material. Supporting notes for each picture, with the relevant attainment target, are included. The books cover nine of the ten themes in this Manual; the unit on moving things is not represented as pictorial source material will not enhance children's first-hand activity at key stage 1.

- **Picture Resource Book 1**
  - Plants
  - Light
  - Sky and weather
- **Picture Resource Book 2**
  - Themselves and others and how to keep healthy
  - Animals
  - How people change the environment
- **Picture Resource Book 3**
  - Sound
  - Materials
  - Batteries, buzzers and bulbs

Science Discussion Books

These have been designed to enhance the development of children's knowledge and understanding of science. Each book contains a carefully selected set of photographs which are linked thematically with accompanying captions and questions.

Section 1
Planning Science

At the heart of good primary practice is learning through first-hand experience. One of the main tasks of the school and the teacher is to plan and present children with the broad range of experiences which will help them develop both their knowledge and understanding of science, and attitudes and skills for its exploration.

Guidance on managing science activities in the classroom offered in section 2, 'Organising Science', which gives a framework for teaching and learning. This section is about devising a coherent curriculum to give all children access to the programme of study, and support to achieve their potential.

Planning and record keeping for key stage 1

Planning a scheme of work to cover the infant years which constitute **key stage 1** will involve schools in ensuring that children have a broad range of opportunities. This range is necessary for them to: cover the programme of study laid down in the **National Curriculum** and demonstrate progression in learning as mapped out by the **attainment targets and levels**.

All children will be working towards attainment target 1, exploration of science, whenever they are engaged in scientific activity. The attainment targets for knowledge and understanding, however, are context related, and the school will need to provide a progressive, broad and balanced range of contexts to give children the full range of learning opportunities they require. This needs careful planning. The following framework is designed to help teachers to accomplish this important planning task.

Science is essentially about **finding out** through first-hand experience. By grouping together knowledge and understanding attainment targets it is possible to arrive at ten 'finding out' themes, each of which holds one or more **units** (See Figure 1).

These themes and units are identifiable aspects of the child's world. Between them they cover the full range of learning opportunities in the programme of study and the full range of knowledge and understanding attainment targets. (See Figure 2)

By using the themes and units as planning units the teacher is released from the task of continually cross-checking coverage of the programme of study. Providing each unit is covered, preferably more than once, during key stage 1 the requirements of the National Curriculum will be met.

This straightforward approach to planning allows the teacher to exploit the potential of a cross-curricular or thematic approach. The teacher can see where in the whole infant curriculum children could naturally be finding out about particular units – for example, in cooking and baking activities, art and craft or play – and can choose topics that will support learning in each unit.

The units also give a basis for **record keeping**. The teacher can use the unit-by-unit photocopiable record sheets and evaluation checklists provided in this manual to record both the potential of each topic, and also the children's actual experiences. A strategy for planning and record keeping is outlined below.

Planning Science

Figure 1 The ten themes and their units

THEME	UNIT
Light	Light, shadows, colours and mirrors
Sound	Sounds
Batteries, buzzers and bulbs	How to make bulbs light and buzzers sound
How people change the environment	Improving the appearance of the local environment
Themselves and others and how to keep healthy	Growing and moving
	Using the senses
	Feeding
Plants	How to take care of plants
	How plant life varies
	Seasonal and daily changes in plants
Animals	How to take care of animals
	How animal life varies
	Seasonal and daily changes in animals
Sky and weather	Changes in the weather and the effect of the weather
	Changes in the sky: light and dark
	Changes in temperature: hot and cold
Moving things	How to make things move
Materials	Natural materials found in the locality: stones, rocks, soil
	Everyday substances which melt and solidify: ice/water, wax, chocolate etc.
	Everyday materials: sand, wood, metal, plastics, paper, clay, fabrics (including magnets)
	Using materials to make structures

Figure 2 Attainment targets covered by each theme

THEME	ATTAINMENT TARGETS FOR KEY STAGE 1												
	1	2	3	4	5	6	9	10	11	12	13	14	15	16
Light	●									●			●	
Sound	●									●	●			
Batteries, buzzers and bulbs	●								●	●				
How people change the environment	●				●					●				
Themselves and others and how to keep healthy	●		●	●						●	●			
Plants	●	●	●							●				●
Animals	●	●	●	●						●				●
Sky and weather	●							●		●	●			●
Moving things	●								●	●	●			
Materials	●					●	●	●	●	●	●			

Planning Science

Using the themes and units

The ten themes and their units can be used by the teacher to plan and implement science in the context of the cross-curricular topics, and to keep records of planning and children's experience.

This section provides a strategy which the school can adopt, beginning by identifying learning outcomes and choosing topics to support them. By following the strategy the school will be able to ensure that during key stage 1 children are provided with a balanced set of science experience which covers the full range of the National Curriculum programme of study and attainment targets.

The section includes:

- an overview of the approach.
- an illustration indicating how one school and one teacher from that school have successfully used this approach to planning and curriculum record keeping.

Overview of the approach

Step 1
- **Select topics.**

As a first step, areas of study should be identified by all teachers in collaboration to use as vehicles for children's learning across the curriculum. These areas of study might be topics, themes or projects (e.g. autumn, clothes) or units of work based on a resource (e.g. cooking, the school pond).

For the sake of simplicity the term 'topic' is used throughout this manual.

Points to consider when choosing topics are:

- the children – their needs and interests, and the appropriateness of the context to their experience and stage of development. Particularly, consider the opportunities the topic could provide for expanding children's awareness of cultural and ethnic diversity.
- the resources – the range and quality of appropriate objects and materials which can be made available for children to handle and work with. Particularly, consider the season, the visits which can be arranged and the stories and poems which can be provided.
- the potential – the scope which the context provides for a wide-ranging selection of activities embracing aspects of mathematics, science, English (writing, reading and speaking and listening), the arts (drama, music, painting, drawing and three-dimensional work), the humanities (history and geography) and technology and design.

Step 2
- **Identify potential for science experiences.**
- **Record potential.**

  Having selected your topics, use the flow-diagram (figure 3) to identify which themes and units are covered by the topics. Record this potential by ticking the themes and units for which each topic has learning opportunities.

Step 3
- **Select from the potential by using the record of science experiences the children have previously been provided with.**
- **Record planning.**

From the potential identified using the flow-diagram, select the themes and

Planning Science

Figure 3 Identifying opportunities

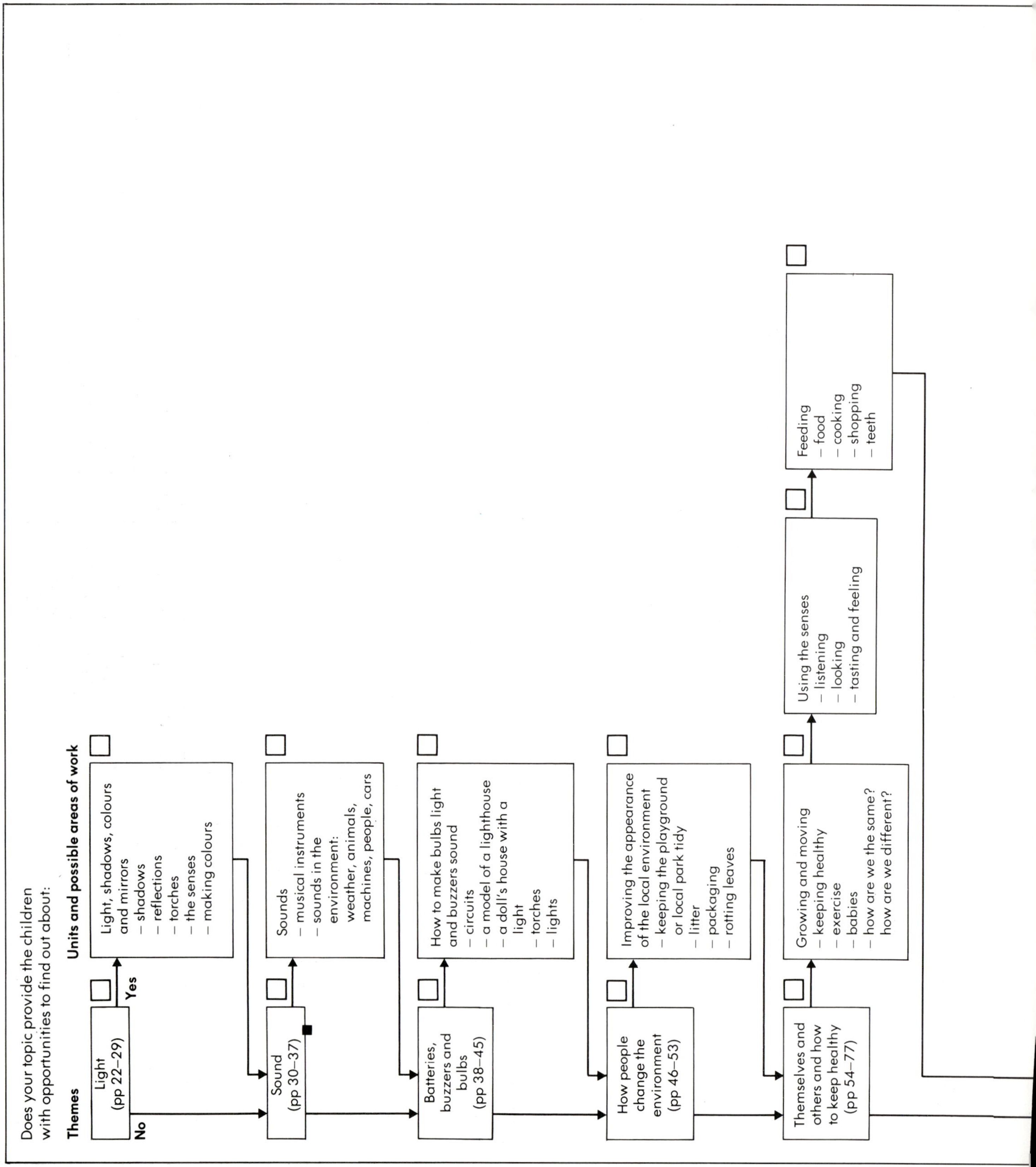

Does your topic provide the children with opportunities to find out about:

Themes	Units and possible areas of work
Light (pp 22–29)	Light, shadows, colours and mirrors – shadows – reflections – torches – the senses – making colours
Sound (pp 30–37)	Sounds – musical instruments – sounds in the environment: weather, animals, machines, people, cars
Batteries, buzzers and bulbs (pp 38–45)	How to make bulbs light and buzzers sound – circuits – a model of a lighthouse – a doll's house with a light – torches – lights
How people change the environment (pp 46–53)	Improving the appearance of the local environment – keeping the playground or local park tidy – litter – packaging – rotting leaves
Themselves and others and how to keep healthy (pp 54–77)	Growing and moving – keeping healthy – exercise – babies – how are we the same? how are we different? Using the senses – listening – looking – tasting and feeling Feeding – food – cooking – shopping – teeth

Flow: Yes → Units; No → next theme.

© Bishop Grosseteste College 1990. Copying permitted for purchasing school only. This material is not 'copyright free'.

Planning Science

Plants (pp 78–105) → How to take care of plants
- growing plants
- germinating seeds
- gardening

→ How plant life varies
- different plants in the local environment
- plants or parts of plants that can be used for food
- plants that grow in different climates
- plants in the garden

→ Seasonal and daily changes in plants
- the life cycle of plants and the seasons
- flowers that close their petals at night

Animals (pp 106–121) → How to take care of animals
- classroom animals: guineapig, rabbit, stick insects
- animals brought into the classroom from the local environment: worms, spiders
- pets
- animals at the zoo
- animals at the circus

→ How animal life varies
- pets
- animals in the classroom
- animals (minibeasts) found in the local environment
- birds

→ Seasonal and daily changes in animals
- pets
- birds
- animals which hibernate

Sky and weather (pp 122–145) → Changes in the weather and the effect of the weather
- weather records: clouds, sun, wind, rain, snow, ice
- wind direction
- how the weather affects their lives: clothes, shelter

→ Changes in the sky: light and dark
- changes in the position of the sun
- shadows
- the night sky: stars, the moon

→ Changes in temperature: hot and cold
- winter and summer
- melting, freezing
- keeping warm
- keeping cool

Moving things (pp 146–153) → How to make things move
- toys which move
- the weather and the wind
- rolling, pulling, pushing
- lifting

Materials (pp 154–183) → Natural materials found in the locality:
- stones, rocks, soil
- stones, sand, rocks, soils
- making models with clay

→ Everyday materials: sand, wood, metal, plastics, paper, clay, fabrics (including magnets):
- making things: models, pictures, collages, musical instruments
- clothes and fabrics
- sorting materials

→ Everyday substances which melt and solidify: ice/water, wax, chocolate etc.
- food cooking: jelly, cakes
- ice, frost, snow

→ Using materials to make structures
- making models bridges, arches, towers, buildings, models which move, musical instruments

© Bishop Grosseteste College 1990. Copying permitted for purchasing school only. This material is not 'copyright free'.

5

units which you will provide children with planned experiences of in your chosen topic.

If this approach is adopted by the whole school it will be possible to build up a school record sheet relating to a particular year group of pupils. This will contain the summative record of the themes and units all teachers have incorporated into their work with the children in different years (see figure 4).

To ensure a balanced coverage it would be valuable to select those themes and units which have not been covered previously. Other points to consider are:

- whether this topic gives the best context for this theme and unit.
- whether this is the best stage of the children's experience at which to present these ideas.
- how your topic will extend the children's experience if it covers units they have visited before.

Having made the selection from the potential you have identified, record this planning on the class record sheet (figure 5).

Step 4
- **Do the planned work in the classroom.**

Step 5
- **Record experiences provided on class record sheet.**
- **Record experiences provided on school record sheet.**

Having completed your topic, record the actual themes and units which the topic incorporated on the class record sheet (figure 5) and transfer this information onto a school record sheet for the year group of children (figure 4).

This school record sheet will be a valuable resource for other teachers who will eventually be able to take account of the work you have done with the children in *their* planning.

Using the 5-step approach

Step 1
A school identified the following as topics to be used as the contexts for cross-curricular work within a year:

- The building site
- Food
- Winter
- An environmental study
  - woodland
  - pond
  - school grounds

Step 2
Figure 6 shows a class record sheet completed by the teacher. Her four topics were spaced out across the year, and she used the sheet to record the science opportunities within these topics as she had identified them using the flow-diagram.

Planning Science

Figure 4 School record sheet

Finding out about . . .		Key stage 1								
		Reception			Year 1			Year 2		
		Autumn	Spring	Summer	Autumn	Spring	Summer	Autumn	Spring	Summer
Light	Light, shadows, colours and mirrors									
Sound	Sounds									
Batteries, buzzers and bulbs	How to make bulbs light and buzzers sound									
How people change the environment	Improving the appearance of the local environment									
Themselves and others and how to keep healthy	Growing and moving									
	Using the senses									
	Feeding									
Plants	How to take care of plants									
	How plant life varies									
	Seasonal and daily changes in plants									
Animals	How to take care of animals									
	How animal life varies									
	Seasonal and daily changes in animals									
Sky and weather	Changes in the weather and the effect of the weather									
	Changes in the sky: light and dark									
	Changes in temperature: hot and cold									
Moving things	How to make things move									
Materials	Natural materials found in the locality: stones, rocks, soil									
	Everyday substances which melt and solidify: ice/water, wax, chocolate etc.									
	Everyday materials: sand, wood, metal, plastics, paper, clay, fabrics (including magnets)									
	Using materials to make structures									

© Bishop Grosseteste College 1990. Copying permitted for purchasing school only. This material is not 'copyright free'.

Planning Science

Figure 5 Class record sheet   Class _____   Year _____

		Autumn term Topics	Spring term Topics	Summer term Topics
Finding out about . . .				
Light	Light, shadows, colours and mirrors			
Sound	Sounds			
Batteries, buzzers and bulbs	How to make bulbs light and buzzers sound			
How people change the environment	Improving the appearance of the local environment			
Themselves and others and how to keep healthy	Growing and moving			
	Using the senses			
	Feeding			
Plants	How to take care of plants			
	How plant life varies			
	Seasonal and daily changes in plants			
Animals	How to take care of animals			
	How animal life varies			
	Seasonal and daily changes in animals			
Sky and weather	Changes in the weather and the effect of the weather			
	Changes in the sky: light and dark			
	Changes in temperature: hot and cold			
Moving things	How to make things move			
Materials	Natural materials found in the locality: stones, rocks, soil			
	Everyday substances which melt and solidify: ice/water, wax, chocolate etc.			
	Everyday materials; sand, wood, metal, plastics, paper, clay, fabrics (including magnets)			
	Using materials to make structures			

© Bishop Grosseteste College 1990. Copying permitted for purchasing school only. This material is not 'copyright free'.

Planning Science

Figure 6 Science opportunities   Class __3__   Year __1990__

Finding out about...		Autumn term Topics		Spring term Topics	Summer term Topics
		The building site	food	Winter	Environmental study
Light	Light, shadows, colours and mirrors				
Sound	Sounds				
Batteries, buzzers and bulbs	How to make bulbs light and buzzers sound	■			
How people change the environment	Improving the appearance of the local environment	■			■
Themselves and others and how to keep healthy	Growing and moving		■		
	Using the senses				
	Feeding		■		
Plants	How to take care of plants				
	How plant life varies	■	■	■	■
	Seasonal and daily changes in plants	■	■	■	■
Animals	How to take care of animals				
	How animal life varies	■	■	■	■
	Seasonal and daily changes in animals	■	■	■	■
Sky and weather	Changes in the weather and the effect of the weather			■	■
	Changes in the sky: light and dark			■	■
	Changes in temperature: hot and cold			■	
Moving things	How to make things move	■			
Materials	Natural materials found in the locality: stones, rocks, soil	■			■
	Everyday substances which melt and solidify: ice/water, wax, chocolate etc.		■		
	Everyday materials; sand, wood, metal, plastics, paper, clay, fabrics (including magnets)	■			
	Using materials to make structures	■			

Planning Science

Step 3

Figure 7 shows the school record sheet the teacher had available to help her plan. She also had the year group's evaluation checklists (see section 3), which gave her detailed information on the range of science activities the children had experienced in reception and year 1. Using this information the teacher

Figure 7 The year group's science experiences

Finding out about...		Key stage 1								
		Reception			Year 1			Year 2		
		Autumn	Spring	Summer	Autumn	Spring	Summer	Autumn	Spring	Summer
Light	Light, shadows, colours and mirrors	■	■	■						
Sound	Sounds		■	■						
Batteries, buzzers and bulbs	How to make bulbs light and buzzers sound									
How people change the environment	Improving the appearance of the local environment					■	■			
Themselves and others and how to keep healthy	Growing and moving	■								
	Using the senses	■	■							
	Feeding	■								
Plants	How to take care of plants	■			■					
	How plant life varies				■	■	■			
	Seasonal and daily changes in plants				■	■				
Animals	How to take care of animals				■	■				
	How animal life varies				■	■	■			
	Seasonal and daily changes in animals				■	■				
Sky and weather	Changes in the weather and the effect of the weather	■	■		■	■		■		
	Changes in the sky: light and dark									
	Changes in temperature: hot and cold									
Moving things	How to make things move	■								
Materials	Natural materials found in the locality: stones, rocks, soil									
	Everyday substances which melt and solidify: ice/water, wax, chocolate etc.				■	■				
	Everyday materials; sand, wood, metal, plastics, paper, clay, fabrics (including magnets)									
	Using materials to make structures					■	■			

Planning Science

selected, from the potential she had identified for each topic, themes and units to complete the balanced coverage of the National Curriculum programme of study across the infant years. She recorded this planning on the class record sheet.

Figure 8 shows how the potential the teacher identified for her four topics related to the previous scientific experience of the children in her class.

Figure 8 Opportunities and previous experience

Finding out about . . .		Key stage 1								
		Reception			Year 1			Years 2		
		Autumn	Spring	Summer	Autumn	Spring	Summer	Autumn	Spring	Summer
Light	Light, shadows, colours and mirrors		■	■						
Sound	Sounds		■							
Batteries, buzzers and bulbs	How to make bulbs light and buzzers sound							■		
How people change the environment	Improving the appearance of the local environment					■	■	■		■
Themselves and others and how to keep healthy	Growing and moving	■								
	Using the senses	■	■							
	Feeding							■		■
Plants	How to take care of plants			■	■					
	How plant life varies				■	■	■		■	
	Seasonal and daily changes in plants							■		
Animals	How to take care of animals	■					■	■	■	
	How animal life varies					■		■		
	Seasonal and daily changes in animals									■
Sky and weather	Changes in the weather and the effect of the weather		■	■				■	■	
	Changes in the sky: light and dark				■					
	Changes in temperature: hot and cold									■
Moving things	How to make things move	■								
Materials	Natural materials found in the locality: stones, rocks, soil							■		■
	Everyday substances which melt and solidify: ice/water, wax, chocolate etc.				■	■			■	
	Everyday materials; sand, wood, metal, plastics, paper, clay, fabrics (including magnets)							■	■	
	Using materials to make structures				■					

Planning Science

A whole-school approach to planning will ensure that teachers are not planning work just to fill gaps. Ideally all children should visit each unit more than once during the infant years. This will need careful, co-ordinated planning for each year group, from reception through to the end of year 2. The approach suggested will help the school to achieve this, and to provide scientific learning experiences in meaningful contexts.

Section 3 of this manual, which offers guidance on implementing science activities in each of themes and units, includes ideas on useful contexts for the work. (If schools have to resort to filling gaps, these suggestions will also be useful.)

Step 4

When she had established the themes and units to incorporate into her topic on the building site, the teacher used section 3 of this manual to plan activities she would engage the children in, and the way in which she would set the activities in context. She:

- selected investigable questions to pursue with her class, using the building site as the context.
- reviewed the Nelson Science materials that support and extend the children's practical enquiry.
- referred to the guidance given on assessment and evaluation, to provide herself with a clear rationale for the work.
- planned a clear sequence of activity and discussion around a framework of:
  – starting points
  – action points
  – review points.

See sections 2 and 3 for detailed guidance.

Step 5

When she had completed the building site topic, the teacher recorded the themes and units it had actually covered on her class record sheet. She transferred this information onto the school record sheet at the end of the term.

The teacher repeated steps 4 and 5 for her other three topics.

Section 2
Organising Science in the Infant Classroom

Thinking about organisation

There is a range of organisational patterns available to the teacher, all of which have advantages and limitations. It is not appropriate to suggest that one organisational method should be used in preference to others. The teacher needs to find a set of preferred working arrangements within the resources available and his/her own experience and professional philosophy. The points that follow may help the teacher in thinking about these arrangements.

Whatever organisational pattern is adopted, it is important that children work in an environment in which real things happen, in which they are given time to pursue a task from start to finish, and in which there is time for them to talk with other children and with the teacher.

One important aspect of organisation is the layout and resourcing of the classroom. The teacher must make certain that the classroom can be addressed as a whole unit or in small working groups. There needs to be sufficient space, furniture, tools, materials and equipment for a variety of individual or group investigations. Provision for quiet learning areas, table-top spaces for investigative work and carefully selected learning resources, textbooks, museum artefacts and plants all contribute to the quality of learning.

Care and attention need to be given to the displaying of children's work, and the teaching environment should be organised for warmth, colour and aesthetic appeal.

The teacher thus needs to organise the material environment, the selection and organisation of artefacts, materials and tools, and the use of space and time. He/she also needs to organise the interpersonal environment. This involves ensuring that children have opportunities to talk and discuss in small groups or with the class, and that the teacher is able to interact and intervene in a meaningful way with individuals and with groups.

Both of these aspects of organisation are crucial if children are to be provided with the right conditions within which to learn.

Scientific attitudes

The National Curriculum does not specify the scientific attitudes and personal qualities which it is hoped children will develop as a result of their work in science. Throughout the infant years, however, children must be provided with encouragement and example so that they develop:

- open-mindedness
- respect for evidence
- curiosity
- sensitivity to the living and non-living environment
- perseverance
- critical reflection
- creativity and inventiveness

Organising Science

Information technology

Figure 2 shows that each of the units can provide a context for attainment target 12: the scientific aspects of information technology including microelectronics. The programme of study for key stage 1 makes it clear that 'Children's normal work in all areas should involve, where appropriate, the use of information sources and computers. When appropriate, they should have the opportunity to use tape recorders and television to broaden their experience of science.'

The use of information technology (IT) includes a range of everyday devices which receive and transfer information: television, radio, tape-recorder/CD player, video, telephone, calculator, digital watch, microwave oven, computer etc. Teachers can provide children with opportunities to develop their general awareness and knowledge of IT by:

- using TV, radio and/or video whenever relevant, and to give experiences that cannot be given first hand.
- showing children how to use cassette tape-recorders to record their investigations.
- discussing the safe use of these electrical devices in everyday life.
- giving children the opportunity to operate TV, radio, telephone etc. under supervision.

The computer in the classroom can be used to support, enhance and extend science activities. **Word processing** can help with and add to the use of scientific language (through software such as Concept Keyboard) and recording and reporting (e.g. through Folio and Prompt Writer). The gathering and handling of information and the interpretation of results can be extended with the use of simple **data handling programs**. Some of these are shown in figure 9.

A framework for teaching and learning

A useful approach to the organisation and management of children's science work is to see it as having a beginning, a middle and an end.

For each of the 21 units we have included suggestions for **starting points** which teachers could use to begin exploration and investigation work. These starting points could be undertaken with a whole class or with groups of different sizes.

The middle part of the sequence is the investigational work which children engage in.

The elements of this – **asking questions, gathering information** and **handling information** – are all **action points.**

The conclusion to the sequence we have termed **review points**. We acknowledge that it is crucial that teachers interact with children during their practical investigations and that talk is the principle means by which teachers mediate children's learning through first-hand experience. We see review points as being those aspects of the children's work which are talked about in a larger group, with the teacher, once the practical part of the investigation is completed for the time being.

Starting points, action points and review points are discussed in detail below.

In addition to starting points, action points and review points each of the 21 units contains:

- guidance on the **topics** and contexts in which the scientific learning opportunities might be appropriately located.

Figure 9 Examples of simple data handling programs

Program	Details	Supplier
Branch	A binary tree database which helps children to see similarities between groups of objects	MESU, Unit 6, Sir William Lyons Road, Science Park, University of Warwick, Coventry CV4 7EZ
Datashow	A simple graphing program which children can use to enter and sort data and see it displayed as a table, bar chart or pie chart	Hoddle, Doyle and Meadow Ltd, Old Head Road, Elsenham, Bishop Stortford, Hertfordshire CS22 6JN
Our Facts	A straightforward database which allows creation and interrogation of files on any topic	
First Facts	An easy-to-use database requiring a minimum of keystrokes to enter and review data	Resource, Exeter Road, Off Coventry Grove, Doncaster, South Yorkshire DN2 4PY

Organising Science

- details of the Nelson Science **classroom materials** which might appropriately support the activities in the unit.
- the possible **related units** which teachers might exploit when planning sequences of work or when responding to the direction in which the children seem to be taking the work.
- advice and guidance on the **resources and equipment** that are likely to be used by children carrying out investigations within the unit.
- advice and guidance to raise awareness about possible **safety** hazards associated with practical work in the unit.
- A photocopiable **evaluation checklist**, summarising in a list of statements the parts of the relevant attainment targets at levels 1-3 which could be covered by the unit. The checklist can be used to help with planning and to record actual experience provided for the children.

We recommend that all schools have copies of the booklet *Be Safe: Some Aspects of Safety in Science and Technology in Primary Schools* (Association for Science Education, 1988).

Starting points

Starting points for the child

The starting points for scientific learning come most effectively from the natural curiosity of the child.

A **classroom environment** of continuous, planned change can challenge this curiosity and invite enquiry. **Classroom displays** are used by many teachers to provide the changing and challenging scene needed. Displays which are well designed, and include materials and artefacts as well as questions which prompt action and thought, not only act as starting points but are also a way of supporting and broadening the work in the classroom.

Other starting points can come from:

- **visits** to building sites, farms, museums, fire stations etc.
- **visits to the school** by police officers, opticians, engineers, vets etc.
- **stories** such as 'The Three Little Pigs', Eric Carle's *The Very Hungry Caterpillar* etc.

The **prior experiences** of the children are crucial here. It is important that the teacher spends time encouraging children to build a context for the investigations they are about to engage in, so that they can own the investigations and not just do them. Children need to have opportunities to talk about their previous experience – their scientific learning as well as their life experiences.

Science is essentially a process in which experiences are not only expanded but also refined into categories. By asking children to think and talk about what they think might happen and what they think they will find out when they undertake an investigation we are helping them to draw on previous experience and thus give a mental context for the work that follows.

Starting points for the teacher

At the start of any exploration in the classroom the teacher must have a clear understanding of the purpose of the children's work and a well-planned set of practical arrangements to make possible the coming together of child, teacher, task and materials. The detailed guidance for each of the 21 units in section 3 is designed to support the teacher in this.

Action points

Action points cover the first-hand practical exploration which the child engages in. They relate specifically to attainment target 1: exploration of science.

The programme of study and the level-by-level statements of attainment for this target provide teachers with a detailed specification of the activity which children need to have opportunities to engage in.

Exploration of science is firmly locked into science knowledge and understanding, providing the vehicle for pupils' developing and changing ideas about scientific phenomena and events, as well as offering them opportunities to acquire particular skills. To help teachers translate the part of the programme of study which relates to exploration of science into action we have divided the process of exploration into three components in the action points (see figure 10).

Finding out about materials and events involves children in:

- **asking questions** and suggesting ideas about materials and events.
- **gathering information** through first-hand experience.
- **handling information** that has been gathered by recording and interpreting findings.

Figure 11 shows how the three components of exploration of science relate to the details of the programme of study.

Figures 12 – 14 show how the statements of attainment at levels 1, 2 and 3 relate to the three components of exploration of science.

Organising Science

Figure 10 Components of the action points

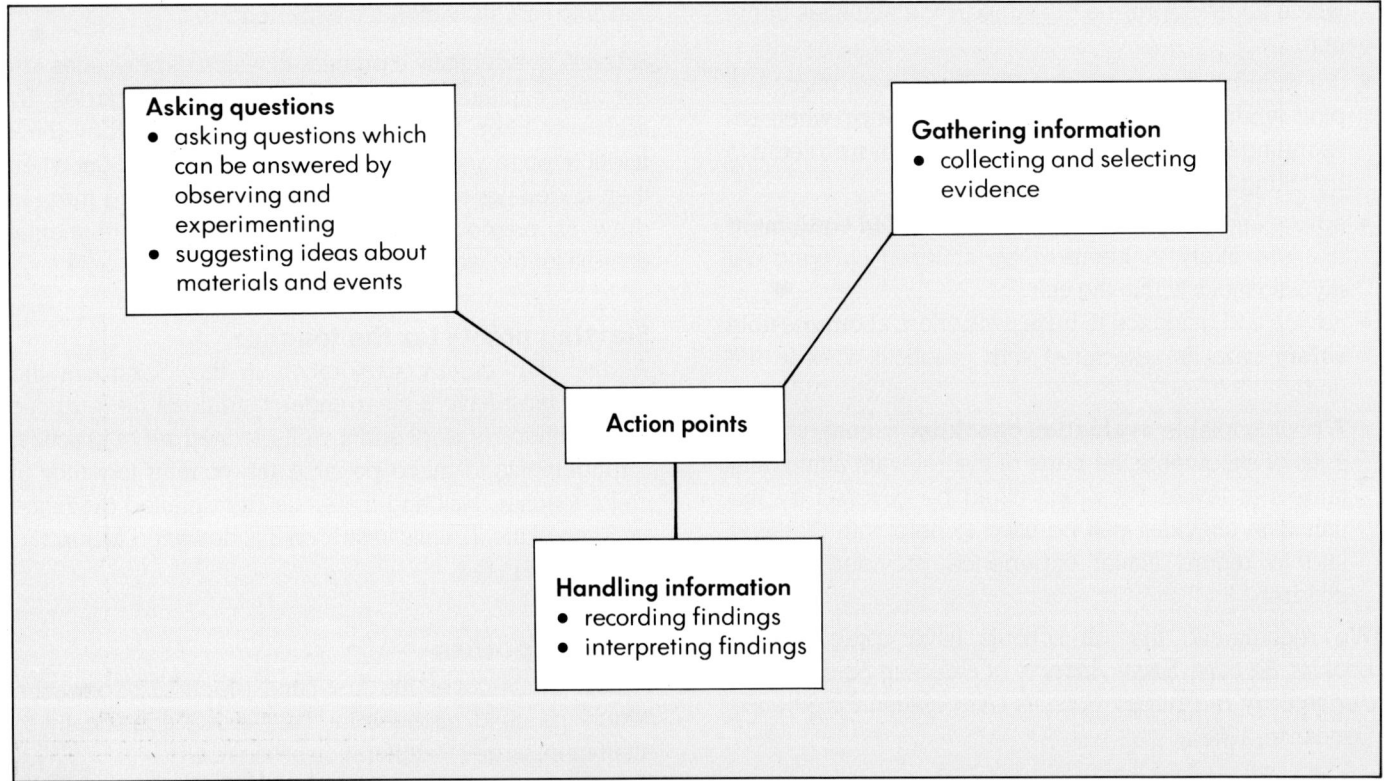

Figure 11 The components and the programmes of study

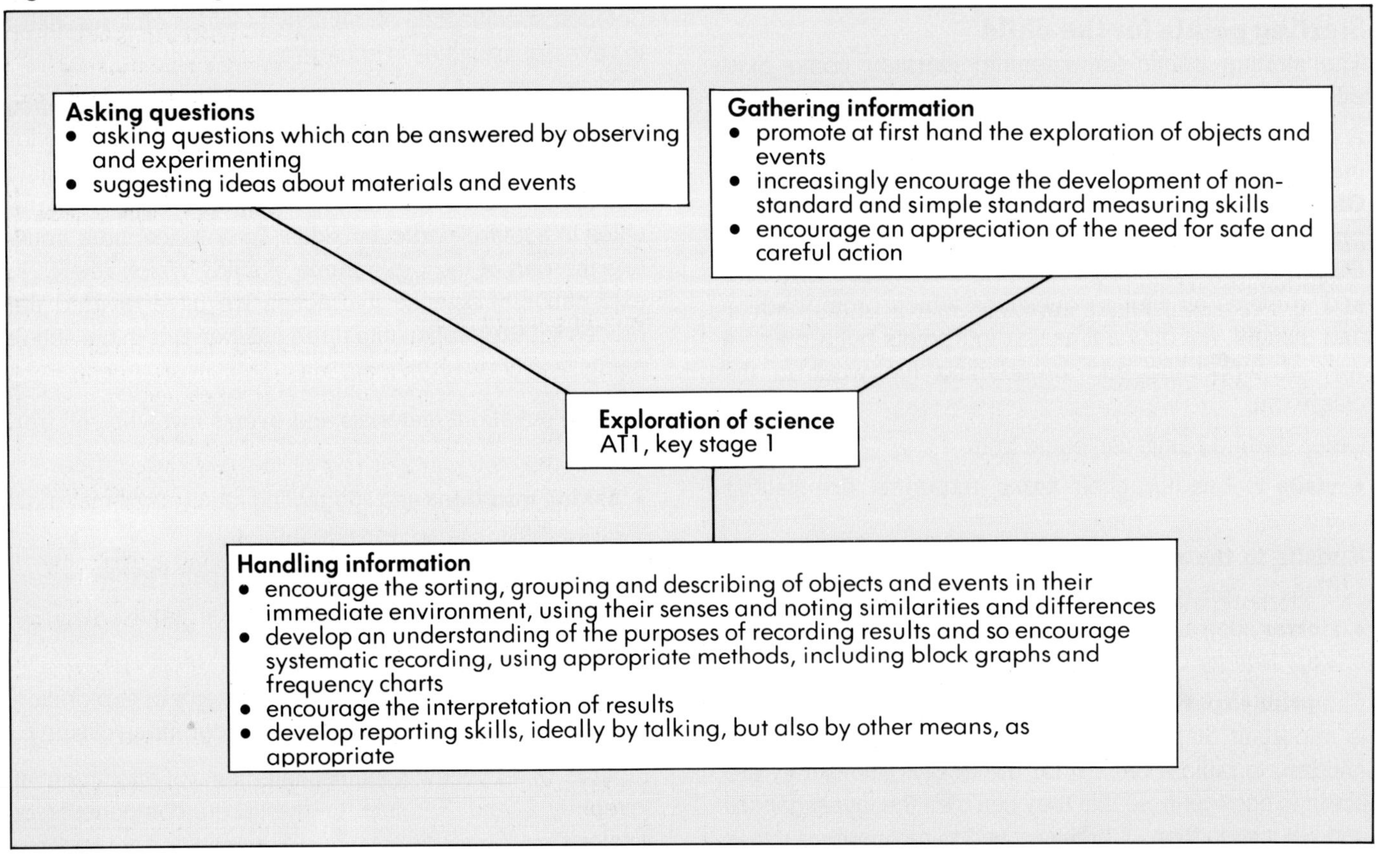

Organising Science

Figure 12 Asking questions: statement of attainment

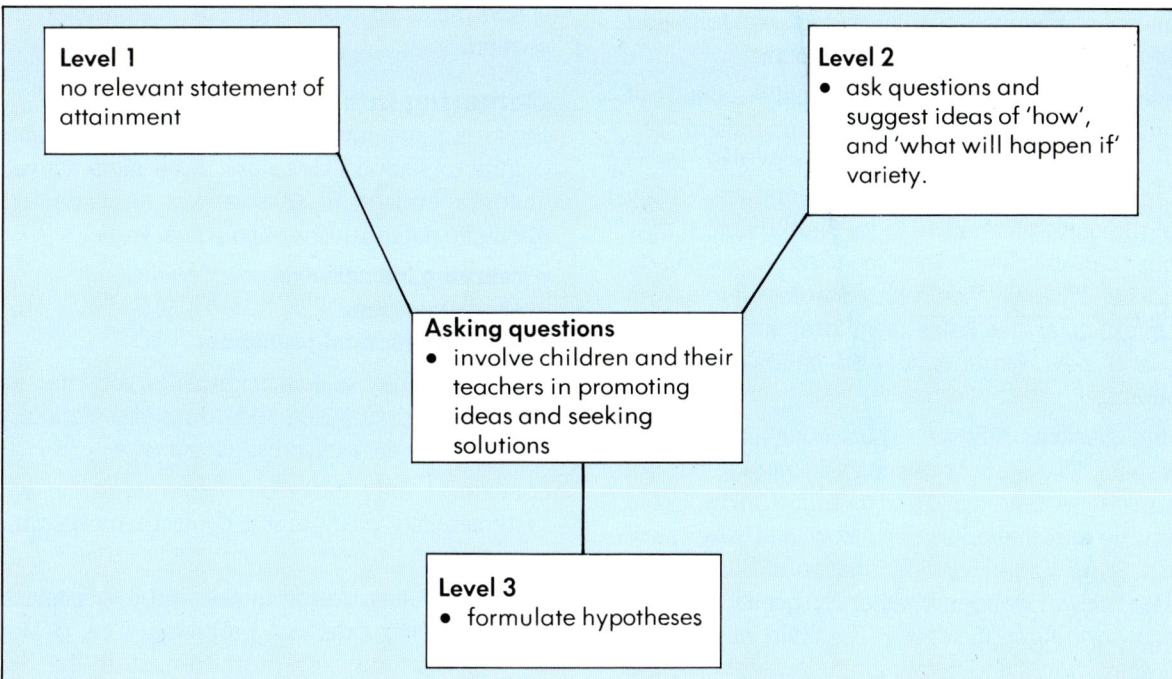

Figure 13 Gathering information: statements of attainment

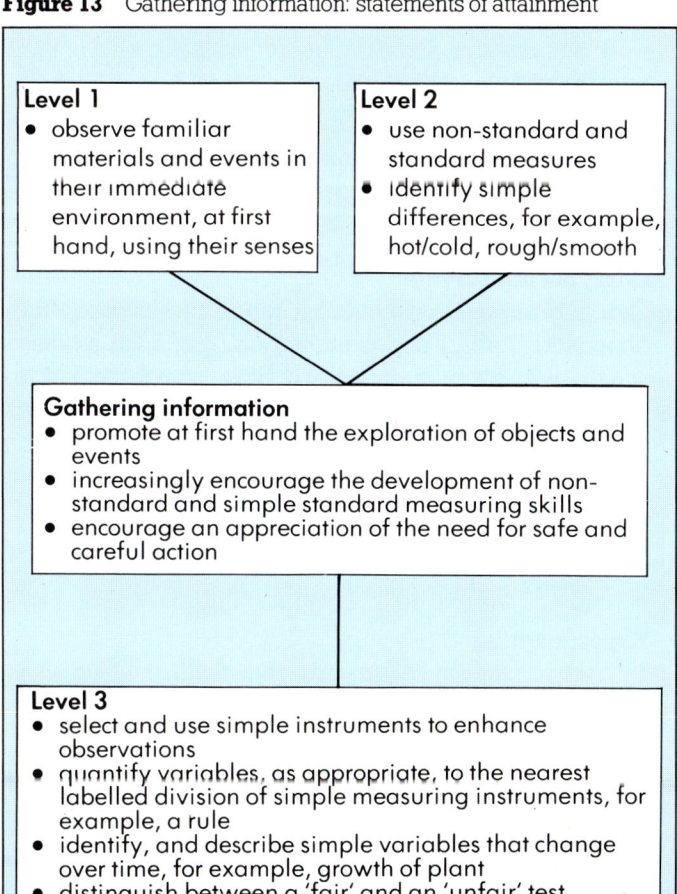

Figure 14 Handling information: statements of attainment

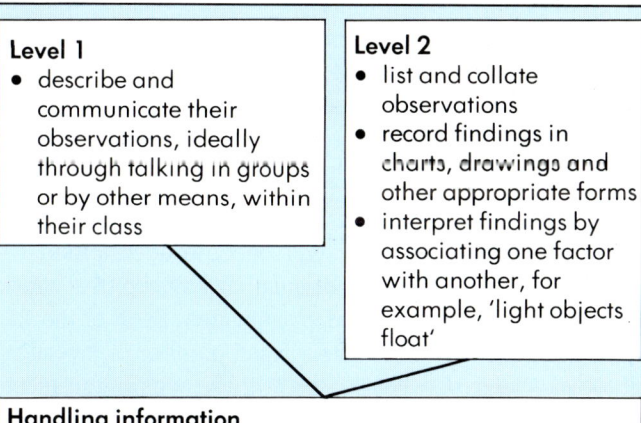

Level 1
- describe and communicate their observations, ideally through talking in groups or by other means, within their class

Level 2
- list and collate observations
- record findings in charts, drawings and other appropriate forms
- interpret findings by associating one factor with another, for example, 'light objects float'

Handling information
- encourage the sorting, grouping and describing of objects and events in their immediate environment, using their senses and noting similarities and differences
- develop an understanding of the purposes of recording results and so encourage systematic recording, using appropriate methods, including block graphs and frequency charts
- encourage the interpretation of results
- develop reporting skills, ideally by talking, but also by other means, as appropriate.

Level 3
- record experimental findings, for example, in tables and bar charts
- interpret simple pictograms and bar charts
- interpret observations in terms of a generalised statement
- describe activities carried out by sequencing the major features

Organising Science

Asking questions

Asking questions is a fundamental part of exploring and developing an understanding of the environment.

Asking questions is the means by which children find out the information they need to help them understand. The questions children ask show where their existing ideas are not adequate to interpret their experiences. They represent the gaps which have to be filled before a new experience can be fitted into or used to challenge existing ideas. Children should be encouraged to ask all kinds of question, as this helps them form links between previous and new experience and so enlarge their understanding.

Many of the questions children ask are complex 'how' and 'why' questions. The teacher needs to encourage this but at the same time help children to frame investigable questions. The explanation-seeking 'how' and 'why' questions need to be turned into information-seeking 'What happens if. . ..' and 'I wonder whether . . .' questions which can be answered through actions. The child will then be able to reach towards understanding by reasoning on the basis of his/her own experience and the evidence from his/her own investigations.

A great many question-forms lead to investigation. For simplicity three forms of question have been selected and used in the material provided for each of the 21 units:

- **I wonder whether. . .**
- **What happens if . . .**
- **Can we find a way to . . .**

We hope that the teacher will become accustomed to using them to exploit the potential for science in a wide and varied range of classroom activities. Each of the 21 units includes only a relatively small number of investigable questions. We have chosen those which link most closely to the National Curriculum programme of study and attainment targets. Many more are clearly possible and it is to be hoped that the teacher and children will generate questions of their own.

The three forms of question we have devised, if used consistently by the teacher, will act as organisers of children's thinking, leading eventually to a questioning approach becoming second nature to the child. For example, a teacher's verbal questions on displays – of objects and materials linked to investigable questions, and of the recordings made by children using investigable questions as the display headings – will help children to formulate their thinking in terms of investigable questions.

There is a clear link between the three kinds of activity which children can engage in to gather information and the three forms of investigable question that prompt and shape these activities. This link is examined in the next section.

Gathering information

Exploring and investigating by gathering information is central to science. There are three main activities which children engage in as scientists to gather information about the natural and technological world:

- **carrying out surveys.**
- **experimenting.**
- **solving practical problems.**

Sometimes they collect information for later interpretation, by observing and recording objects and events in the environment – carrying out surveys.

Sometimes they carry out experiments in which they systematically change and control variables in order to test ideas.

Sometimes they design, make and test artefacts or products—solving practical problems. This designing and making aspect makes a contribution to the **design and technology** component of the National Curriculum as well as providing valuable opportunities for pupils to work out, practise and develop important aspects of their science knowledge and understanding.

The activities in each of the 21 units which make up comprise section 3 of this guide are divided into carrying out surveys, experimenting and solving practical problems.

Carrying out surveys

Carrying out surveys covers a range of activities, from observing, sorting and grouping objects, such as those which have shiny surfaces and those which do not, to observing and recording changes in the weather. Carrying out a survey involves children in observing and recording the key characteristics of objects and events. It involves them in looking for relationships.

'I wonder whether. . .' questions lead children to carry out surveys.

Experimenting

By carrying out simple experiments children can discover the relationship between what they do and the reaction of the thing they handle. **'What happens if . . .' questions** lead children to experiment. Unlike 'I wonder whether. . .' questions, these involve the child in changing variables and observing effects.

Solving practical problems

Practical problems can be used to provide the stimulus and motivation for carrying out surveys and ex-

Organising Science

perimenting. Children can build up the necessary knowledge and understanding through pursuing 'I wonder whether . . .' and 'What happens if . . .' questions. These resources can then be used to solve practical problems.

'Can we find a way to . . .' questions lead children to try to solve real, practical problems.

Handling information

Children's scientific activities should give them opportunities to use and develop a range of communication skills and techniques. In addition to the oral work before, during and after practical activity, children will be involved in making records of their findings through drawings, charts, three dimensional models, and the written word.

A variety of the symbolic codes we all use – written language, numbers, maps, diagrams, graphs etc. – should be presented in the classroom. Children can get information from these, and use them as models. Children should be encouraged to develop their own means of communication and to recognise what might be the most useful means of recording in a particular situation.

Each of the 21 units includes examples of ways in which children can appropriately record findings. The examples given are closely related to the National Curriculum programmes of study, and to science attainment target 1 (exploration of science) and the mathematics attainment target associated with data handling. The examples show teachers how the units' knowledge and understanding content can give a context for particular forms of recording. They do not extend to the whole range of recording methods, which, if used appropriately, can enhance children's experience.

The growth of scientific knowledge and understanding hopefully includes a sense of wonder. A child may need to communicate this response through painting, drawing and poetry. Model making, drama, photography, tape-recording etc. can also be useful ways of helping children to represent their science experiences.

The recording of findings using the written word is not addressed in each of the units. Children can be encouraged to write about what they have done and what they have found out by using single words, lists of observations and possibly more lengthy pieces of chronological and non-chronological writing. Whilst it is important not to overdo written work, children should be helped to become accustomed to and proficient in using words. Their written records will develop gradually from the expressive, where self is the most important, towards transactional writing, which is factual and sequential. The Nelson Science *Science Explorers* books provide frameworks to structure children's written records, as well as to support records in the form of pictures and charts.

Children's investigations will frequently require them to use skills, both intellectual and manipulative, that they do not have, or that they have not developed sufficiently for the task in hand, or that they possess but do not realise the importance, necessity or desirability of using in a particular context. It is our view that specific skills should be taught, extended and/or encouraged when they are needed for specific activities. In this way children will see the value of developing such skills and see their place in science as a means to an end and not as an end in themselves. Such training can be given to small groups of children as their investigatory activities demand, or as lessons for the whole class.

Review points

It is important that children are provided with opportunities for thinking as well as doing. Discussion is therefore vital, as it provides a means of:

- helping children to make links between ideas and experiences and to develop further ideas through talking and sharing thoughts with other children and the teacher.
- helping children to reflect critically on their work to consider how investigations might be improved.

Discussion can also help children to consolidate classroom experience, fit this experience into their mental world and relate it to the real world as they experience it.

Children need to have extensive opportunities to apply and extend their language skills in the context of science work in the classroom. This will foster speaking and listening skills as well as scientific knowledge and understanding.

Evaluation

Teaching a group of busy children leaves little time for involvement in complex evaluation procedures. It is nevertheless important for teachers to spend some time in considering in detail the value of particular sequences of work. To ensure that the quality of classroom practice is maintained we need to be constantly asking questions such as:

- Are all the children being provided with the learning opportunities which we intended?
- Did the children become interested and involved in the topic or unit?
- Did they think about their investigations and attempt to relate what they found out to their previous experiences?

- Are all the children making use of the opportunities and what benefits are they deriving from them?

Asking and answering questions such as these helps us to link learning outcomes to the factors in the classroom which influence that learning.

Opportunities for learning

Each of the 21 units starts with a list of learning opportunities the unit can provide. These lists have been devised by drawing on relevant sections of the programmes of study and relevant attainment targets.

By checking these lists against curricular provision, teachers will be able to assure themselves that children are being provided with the range of learning opportunities prescribed by the National Curriculum.

Learning outcomes

Assessment is an essential part of teaching. Not only must teachers evaluate the extent to which individual children are being provided with particular kinds of learning opportunity, they must also monitor the progress in learning which is taking place as a result.

For most areas of the primary curriculum, not least in science, assessment has been an intuitive activity, part of what each teacher considers as his/her personal professional expertise. It has been clear for some time that this professionalism needs to be made more explicit and shared if the opportunities for each child's progression in learning are to be enhanced. Sharing assumes that the participants have developed agreements on the nature and direction of progress in learning. The National Curriculum attainment targets and levels provide the explicit map of progression on which children's current capability and their progress can be charted.

Elaborate assessment procedures are not very practical in the classroom and children's learning can largely be assessed informally, though systematically. This is likely to be through on-going observation of children at work, through participating in an individual child's experience and through interacting with the child by discussing experience. This formative type of assessment, which provides continuous feedback on the changes in children's ideas and skills over time, can help the teacher to recognise capability and so match work more closely to children's development and needs.

Each of the 21 units in section 3 ends with a photocopiable evaluation checklist which specifies the relevant attainment targets for a series of detailed assessment statements. The use of these checklists is outlined below.

How to use the evaluation checklists

The teacher can use the evaluation checklist which is at the end of each unit as:

- a pre-activity checklist to ensure that activities are developed with a purpose. The statements in the checklist should help sharpen the focus of work in the classroom so that it offers children opportunities to achieve particular attainment levels.
- a post-activity checklist to make and record evaluations of the teaching and learning.

Each of the statements in the list has its own box which the teacher can use for recording.

The checklist is not designed to be a substitute for recording the attainment of individual children. It is, however, a useful means of focusing on the statements of attainment which relate to the unit and of recording those statements which have been used for assessment purposes.

An evaluation checklist covering attainment target 12, the scientific aspects of information technology including microelectronics, is also included at the end of section 3.

Section 3
Science Units

How to use this section

This section gives detailed guidance for each of the 21 units. They are grouped by theme, and every unit has the **theme symbol** on each page. Each unit follows the pattern shown in figure 15.

Colour coding stresses the links between the three types of question in the 'Asking questions' component, and the three types of activity in the investigations and further investigations.

Each unit finishes with a photocopiable evaluation checklist which the teacher can use for planning work and for recording actual experience and attainment.

At the end of this section is an evaluation checklist for attainment target 12: the scientific aspects of information technology including microelectronics. Work relating to this AT can be integrated into the 21 units.

Figure 15 Using each unit

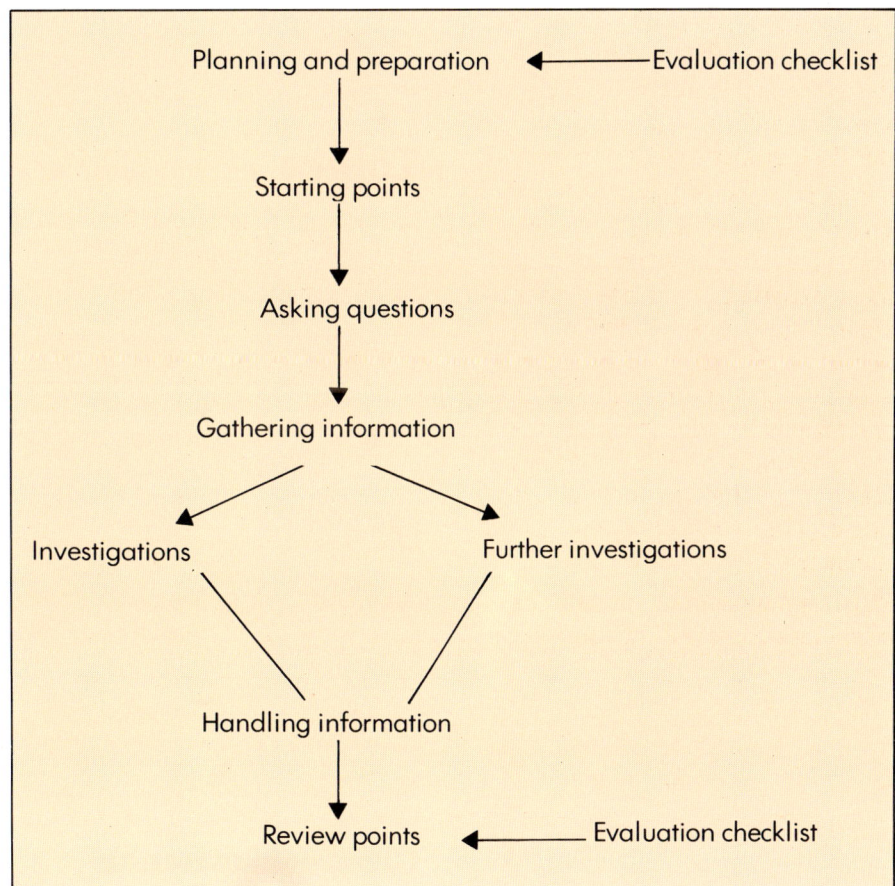

LIGHT

UNIT 1
LIGHT, SHADOWS, COLOURS AND MIRRORS

Opportunities for learning

The range of suggestions in this unit provides children with the following opportunities from the **programme of study** for key stage 1:

- to explore a variety of light sources and effects related to shadows, reflections and colour
- to develop their investigative skills and understanding of science in the context of explorations and investigations

The suggestions for practical activities and discussion outlined in this unit provide children with the experiences necessary to facilitate attainment up to level 3.

Topics

Many topics provide children with opportunities for finding out about light, shadows, colours and mirrors.

Some examples are:

OURSELVES	Sense of sight
WEATHER	Shadows Reflections Sources of light
BUILDINGS	Mirrors Materials with reflective surfaces
SEASONS	Shadows Colour
FESTIVALS	Sense of sight Sources of light Colour

The flow-diagram in section 1 (figure 3, pp.4–5) will help you identify further topics.

Classroom materials

The following Nelson Science materials support this unit:

Picture Resource Book 1

- p.12 – short shadows
- p.13 – long shadows
- p.14 – changing position of the sun

Science Discussion Books for key stage 1

- finding out about light

Planning and Preparation

Science Explorers
- Science Explorer, Carrying Out Surveys 1
- Science Explorer, Experimenting 1
- Science Explorer, Problem Solving 1

Related units

Children may ask questions which will provide opportunities for finding out about the content of other units. For example:

- How to make bulbs light and buzzers sound – Unit 3
- using the senses – Units 6
- changes in the sky: light and dark – Unit 15
- everyday materials: sand, wood, metal, plastics, paper, clay, fabrics (including magnets) – Unit 20

Resources and equipment

- a range of open and close-weave, translucent and opaque fabrics, such as cotton, linen, hessian, wool and nylon
- a range of other materials which are transparent, translucent, opaque and reflective – clear and coloured plastic and glass, for example
- a range of objects with reflective surfaces – spoons, mirrors and saucepan lids, for example
- a range of light sources such as torches, light bulbs and lamps

In the Classroom

Getting started

Starting points

Work on light, shadows, colours and mirrors can arise from:

children talking about:
- special or favourite colours
- days when they have a shadow
- torches and other toys with a light source

children looking closely at:
- a selection of materials – transparent, translucent, opaque

children making collections of:
- coloured artefacts
- a variety of objects that give artificial light such as torches, lamps and bulbs

Asking questions

The activities outlined above could lead to questions such as:

I wonder whether. . .
- we can see the sun every day?
- we can see our reflections in all materials?
- some colours show up better at a distance?
- our shadows in the playground are the same size and shape all through the day?

What happens if . . .
- different coloured paints are mixed together?
- we make shadows in the classroom and change the position of the light source?
- two mirrors are held close together?

Can we find a way to . . .
- stop the sun shining onto a work surface?
- make a dark corner or area lighter?
- make colours lighter or darker?
- make shadow puppets?
- use mirrors to see the back of our heads?
- make a periscope?
- make a kaleidoscope?

Gathering information

Encourage children to think of ways of **gathering information** to help answer these questions.

Investigations which might follow these questions are outlined on pp26–28.

Ideas for taking these investigations further are given below.

Further investigations

Carrying out surveys

Collecting information about:
- the sun as a source of light
– compare the sun in summer with the sun in winter
– observe the sunniest place in the playground or classroom
– observe the position of the sun at different times of day
– observe changes in the weather
- the shadows created on a sunny day
– look at length and shape of shadows
– compare shadows in winter and summer
– observe and measure shadows during the day
- materials, surfaces and reflections
– sort shiny and non-shiny surfaces
– classify reflective and non-reflective surfaces
– sort materials which are transparent or opaque
– observe colours which can be easily seen

Experimenting

- mixing paints and making different colours
– make shade variations of one colour
– mix rainbow colours from primary colours
– make spinners with different colours in different sections
- making shadows in the classroom with torches
– make cardboard shapes to cast different shadows, such as star, diamond, rectangle
– make shadows of different sizes
– make silhouettes of friends
- using mirrors and making reflections
– observe letters of the alphabet which change and do not change in a mirror
– make half shapes and pictures to produce symmetrical patterns and pictures
– count the number of images of a toy seen in two mirrors facing each other
– observe reflections in convex and concave mirrors, or on shiny surfaces like a spoon
– observe curved mirrors which make things look bigger or smaller
– reflect sunlight with a mirror

In the Classroom

Solving practical problems
- creating home environments
– use colour or fabric for a brighter environment
– shade a light source
- using mirrors
– seeing behind, or round corners
- making colours lighter or darker
– use a light source
– mix together coloured paints
– observe colour from a distance

Handling information

Recording findings

Encourage the children to think about ways in which their findings can be recorded.

Talk with the children about your reasons for choosing a particular method of recording.

Findings from practical problem-solving activities can be recorded through drawing and writing.

Findings from surveys and experiments can be recorded individually or as a group by:
- using simple charts and pictograms
- using tables and bar charts

Interpreting findings

Encourage children to link findings and observations and thus try to establish and express cause-and-effect relationships.

Help children to link the position of the light source with the shape and size of shadows, and help them towards the knowledge that the higher the light source the shorter the shadow.

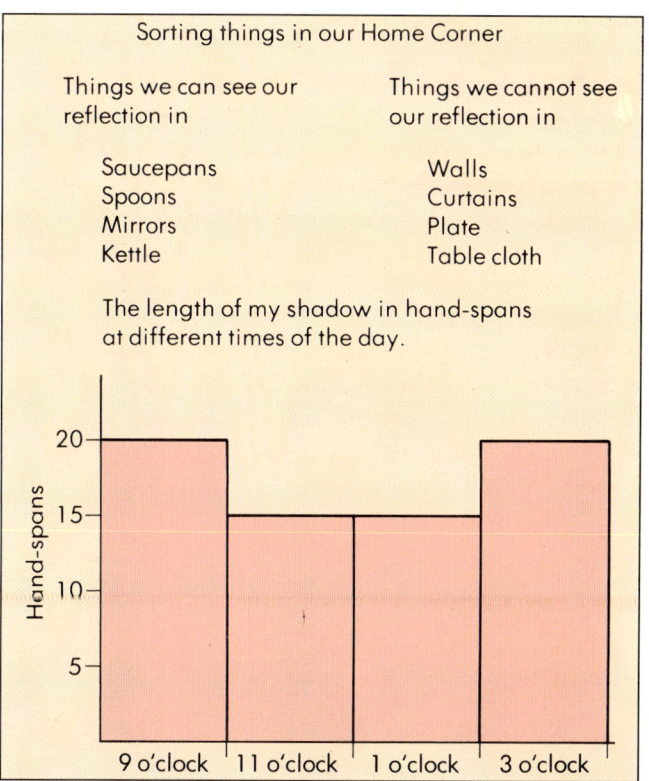

25

In the Classroom

Review points
The following are useful talking points:

Our investigations
- the questions we asked
- how we planned
- how we collected information
- how and why we recorded
- what we found out

Making connections
- the use of light sources in **different occupations and places**, such as mines, caves, lighthouses and dental surgeries
- the need for and usage of colour in **furnishings in the home**, such as curtains, lampshades and walls
- the use of **mirrors and reflective surfaces**, such as dentists' mirrors, torches etc.

Safety
Ensure that the children do not:
- look directly at the sun, even through transparent or coloured materials
- look at very bright lights such as projector beams
- cut themselves on glass
- use glass mirrors during an investigation

Investigations
I wonder whether . . .
- we can see the sun every day?

By looking at the sky in a systematic way, either from a window or from a place in the playground, children can make **detailed observations** of days on which the sun is visible in the sky and days when it is not visible, and **collect information** about bright and dull days.

- we can see our reflections in all materials?

By **looking closely** at a number of different objects made from different materials, children can begin to **classify** broadly those materials in which we can see our reflection and those materials in which we cannot.

Children may also notice other interesting details in their reflections such as the distortion of the image.

- some colours show up better at a distance?

Children can begin to discriminate between colours and recognise their usefulness or otherwise.

They could then **link** these observations with the use of colour in the environment, such as road safety signs, brightly coloured clothes worn by police or ambulance attendants and animal camouflage.

- our shadows in the playground are the same size and shape all through the day?

By **observing** the shape and size of

one child's shadow, and then drawing around the shadow at different times during the day, children can **gather information** about how and why the shape and size of shadows change.

Children could also collect information about how and why the position of a shadow changes.

Encourage the children to measure wherever appropriate, using non-standard and simple standard measuring skills.

In the Classroom

What happens if . . .

- **different coloured paints are mixed together?**

Children can mix together the primary colours of powdered or ready-mixed paint. By varying the quantities of one or more colours they could also experiment with different shades of colour.

- **we make shadows in the classroom and change the position of the light source?**

With a strong artificial light source (a slide or overhead projector, for example) projected onto a white or light-coloured wall, children can **create** silhouettes and shadows.

By moving the light source, children could **compare and measure** the different shadow effects.

Perhaps children might also want to keep the light source static, but move their position in relation to the wall and light source.

- **two mirrors are held close together?**

Children can **compare** the reflected images of objects, such as beads or shells, by altering the positions of the two mirrors. They can obtain different images by holding the mirrors at different angles, or by holding the mirrors in parallel.

Can we find a way to . . .

- **stop the sun shining onto a work surface?**

Children can use different fabrics to act as blinds or curtains at a window.

Alternatively they could **experiment** by using different fabrics and materials in their models to block out an artificial light source.

- **make a dark corner area lighter?**

By **sorting and discriminating** between colours of paper or fabric children can determine which material is most suited to creating a light environment in the classroom or home.

- **make colours lighter or darker?**

Children can **experiment** with coloured paper, or acetate or sweet wrappers. They could mix together the primary colours in paint and then add different amounts of white or black paint.

In the Classroom

- **make shadow puppets?**

Children can **create** their own shadow puppets from black paper. An overhead projector screen could be used, or a screen could be made by using greaseproof paper or white acetate sheeting.

A strong artificial light source, such as an overhead projector light or a powerful lamp, could be substituted for the sun.

- **use mirrors to see the back of our heads?**

Children can use a number of mirrors to solve this problem.

The distance between each mirror and the child's head could be **measured**.

- **make a periscope?**

A simple periscope can be **made** by attaching a mirror to a ruler with a bulldog clip, as shown.

More sophisticated structures could be made by using more than one mirror in a model made from stiff card.

- **make a kaleidoscope?**

A simple kaleidoscope can be **made** by standing two mirrors with their edges touching. Small counters or shells can be placed between them.

The angle of the mirrors could be changed to alter the images.

By adding a third mirror across the ends of the other two, a more complex kaleidoscope could be created. The mirrors could become part of a kaleidoscope model, made from stiff card.

Evaluation Checklist

Unit .... Date ....

Teaching
Have the children been provided with opportunities to:

- work on questions or problems which they have accepted as their own? ☐

AT15
- work on questions or problems which have enabled them to:
  - explore and talk about a variety of light sources? ☐
  - discriminate between and match colours? ☐
  - explore and investigate a range of materials to see if light passes through them? ☐
  - explore how to make shadows and talk about how to change the size and shape of shadows? ☐
  - draw pictures of their investigations with shadows? ☐
  - explore and investigate the formation of images on shiny surfaces? ☐
  - explore and investigate how light can be made to change direction? ☐
  - carry out investigations with mirrors and talk about their findings? ☐

Has the work pupils were engaged in allowed them to:

AT1 • talk about the purposes of recording results? ☐

AT1 • record results by drawing pictures, drawing block graphs and completing frequency charts, tables and bar charts? ☐

AT1 • sort and group objects and events, such as:
  - materials which allow light to pass through and those which do not? ☐
  - materials which have reflective surfaces and those which do not? ☐

AT1 • measure using non-standard and simple standard measuring skills, for instance, how far away we can stand and still read what the sign says in the mirror? ☐

AT1 • distinguish between a fair and an unfair test? ☐

AT1 • interpret findings by linking variables? ☐

AT1 • describe activities carried out by sequencing the major features? ☐

AT1 • discuss their observations and ideas with other children? ☐

AT1 • describe the best way of recording their activities? ☐

AT1 • relate their findings to previous ideas and experiences? ☐

AT1 • reflect upon how their procedures might be improved? ☐

Learning
Have the children demonstrated that they can:

Level 1
AT15 • describe the places that light can come from, such as the sun, lamps, the moon? ☐

AT15 • discriminate between colours and match them? ☐

AT1 • make observations and talk about them? ☐

Level 2
AT15 • describe how shadows are formed? ☐

AT15 • give some examples of materials which light passes through and some of materials which light does not pass through? ☐

AT15 • draw pictures which include colour, light and shade? ☐

AT1 • identify simple variables such as light/dark, bright/dull, transparent/opaque? ☐

AT1 • ask questions and suggest ideas of the 'how' and 'why' variety? ☐

AT1 • measure using non-standard and standard units? ☐

AT1 • record findings in charts and drawings? ☐

AT1 • list and collate observations? ☐

AT1 • interpret findings by associating one factor with another, such as the position of the light source affecting the shadow? ☐

Level 3
AT15 • explain how to make light change direction using mirrors? ☐

AT15 • talk about mirrors and shiny surfaces and indicate an understanding that shiny surfaces can form images? ☐

AT15 • give an account of an investigation with mirrors? ☐

AT1 • formulate hypotheses? ☐

AT1 • distinguish between a fair and an unfair test? ☐

AT1 • measure using simple measuring instruments, such as a ruler to the nearest labelled division? ☐

AT1 • record findings in tables and bar charts? ☐

AT1 • describe activities carried out by sequencing the major features? ☐

AT1 • interpret findings in terms of a generalised statement, such as 'the higher the light source the shorter the shadow'? ☐

© Bishop Grosseteste College 1990. Copying permitted for purchasing school only. This material is not 'copyright free'.

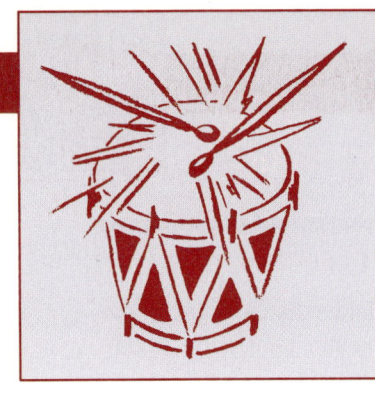

SOUNDS

UNIT 2
SOUNDS

Opportunities for learning

The range of suggestions in this unit provides children with the following opportunities from the **programme of study** for key stage 1:

- to explore a variety of sound-making materials and instruments
- to experience different sounds around them and to find out about their causes and uses
- to develop their investigative skills and understanding of science in the context of explorations and investigations

The suggestions for practical activities and discussion outlined in this unit provide children with the experiences necessary to facilitate attainment up to level 3.

Topics

Many topics provide children with opportunities for finding out about sounds. Some examples are:

SOUND	Sense of hearing Sounds made by different materials
THE WEATHER	Sounds made by rain, hail and thunder
ROAD SAFETY	Cause and use of sound in the environment
MAKING MUSIC	Sounds generated in different materials by striking, plucking, shaking and blowing Sounds made by different musical instruments

The flow-diagram in section 1 (figure 3, pp4–5) will help you identify further topics.

Classroom Materials

The following Nelson Science materials support this unit:

Picture Resource Book 3

- p1 – range of musical instruments
- p2 – vibration in musical instruments
- p3 – sources of sound in the town
- p4 – sources of sound in the country

Science Discussion Books for key stage 1

- finding out about sound

Science Explorers

- **Science Explorer, Carrying Out Surveys 1**
- **Science Explorer, Experimenting 1**
- **Science Explorer, Problem Solving 1**

Planning and Preparation

Related units
Children may ask questions which will provide opportunities for finding out about the content of other units. For example:

- using the senses – unit 6
- changes in the weather and the effect of the weather – unit 14
- everyday materials: sand, wood, metal, plastics, paper, clay, fabrics (including magnets) – unit 20

Resources and equipment
- a variety of materials in different sizes and shapes; for example, wood, metal, paper, plastic and elastic bands
- a variety of containers, for example, cups, bottles, jars, boxes and cardboard tubes
- objects for putting into shakers, such as rice, dried peas, lentils, seeds and paperclips
- a range of junk material, such as cutlery, chains, pans and rubber or plastic tubing
- a selection of musical instruments, for example, guitar, drum, recorder and trumpet

In the Classroom

Getting started

Starting points
Work on sounds can arise from:

children talking about:
- sounds that they can hear
- sounds which frighten them or make them feel safe
- warning sounds with which they are familiar, such as the school bell, a fire alarm, the pelican crossing
- their own toys which make distinctive sounds

children looking closely at, or listening carefully to:
- a range of musical instruments
- different pieces of music both instrumental and vocal
- the wind and the rain

children making collections of:
- different musical instruments
- a variety of sound-makers both natural and manufactured

children visiting:
- a church
- a castle
- an organ loft
- a concert
- an audiometrician

Asking questions
The activities outlined above could lead to questions such as:

> **I wonder whether . . .**
> - some sounds are clearer to hear than others?
> - one instrument can make many sounds?
> - the volume of the sound can be changed?
> - sounds are clearer when we are blindfolded?

> **What happens if . . .**
> - an object is dropped onto different surfaces?
> - an object is shaken, scraped, tapped or blown into?

> **Can we find a way to . . .**
> - change the sounds made by plucking an instrument?
> - make a shaker, as a musical instrument?
> - make up a simple tune?
> - make sounds quieter?

Gathering information

Encourage children to think of ways of **gathering information** to help answer these questions.

Investigations which might follow these questions are outlined on pp.34–36.

Ideas for taking these investigations further are given below.

Further investigations

> **Carrying out surveys**
> **Collecting information about:**
> - **different musical instruments**
> – observe, sort and group instruments for a number of different criteria
> - **various sounds made by musical instruments**
> – find how to get sounds from different musical instruments
> - **how well different sounds can be heard**
> – listen to different sounds around the classroom
> – try to hear sounds through different things
> – stand increasing distances from a sound to find out whether it can still be heard
> - **the number of different sounds which can be heard**
> – observe sounds such as birds, cars, singing, and how they change during the day
> – observe whether everyday sounds change with the weather or the seasons
> - **the most appropriate material for making certain sounds**
> – try to make a sound like the rain
> – try to make a sound like the waves

> **Experimenting**
> - **dropping objects onto different materials**
> – vary the objects, the materials and the height from which they are dropped
> - **using different beaters on percussion instruments**
> – compare what happens with metal, wooden and plastic beaters
> – use a beater to muffle the sound
> - **putting seeds on a drum-skin**
> – observe what happens to the seeds when the drum is tapped or beaten
> – compare what happens to small seeds such as cress and large seeds such as conkers

In the Classroom

> **Solving practical problems**
> - **creating a quiet corner or corridor**
> – observe what effect carpet or curtains have on the sounds which are heard
> – compare how noisy different shoes are
> - **constructing a device which will make enough sound to inform other classes that it is lunch time**
> – measure how far the sound will need to travel
> – compare the effects of using different materials

Handling information

Recording findings

Encourage the children to think about ways in which their findings can be recorded.

Talk with the children about your reasons for choosing a particular method of recording.

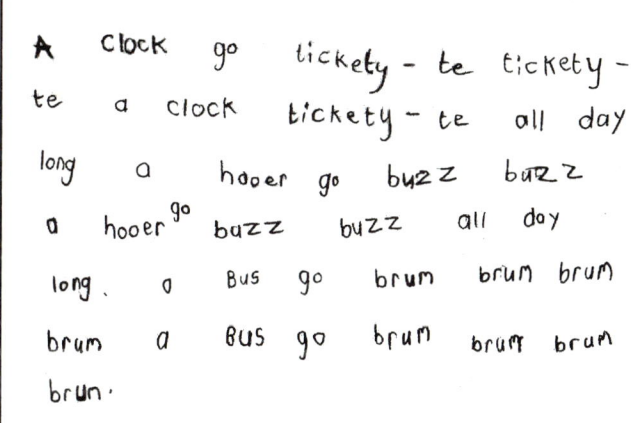

Findings from practical problem-solving activities can be recorded through drawing and writing.

Findings from surveys and experiments can be recorded individually or as a group by:

- using simple charts and pictograms
- using tables and bar charts

Interpreting findings

Encourage children to link findings and observations, and thus try to establish and express cause-and-effect relationships.

Help children to be aware that sound is heard when the sound reaches the ear.

Review points

The following are useful talking points:

Our investigations
- the questions we asked
- how we planned

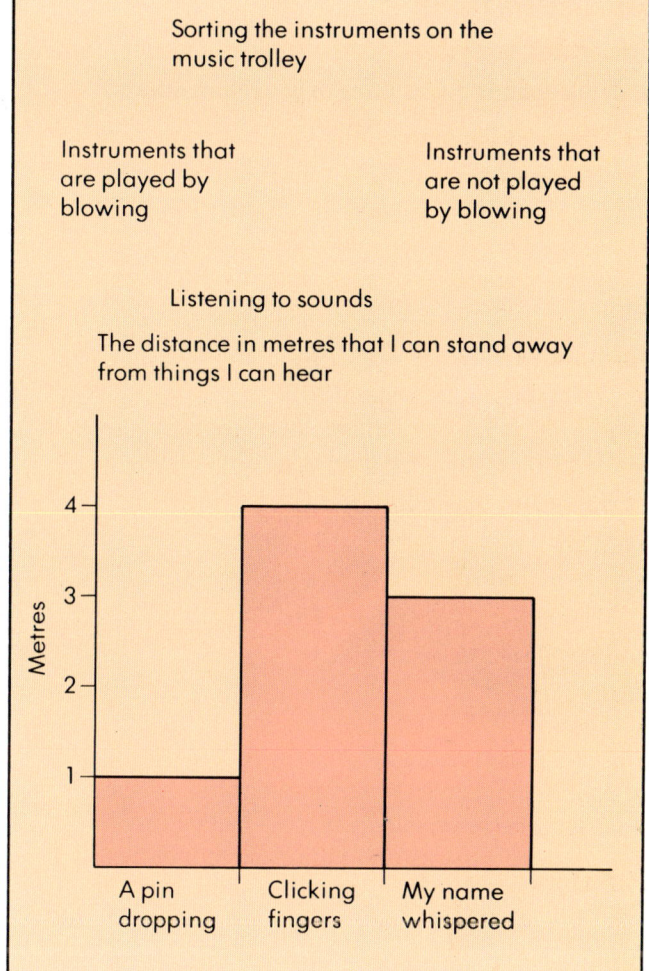

- how we collected information
- how and why we recorded
- what we found out

Making connections
- the use of sounds for **warning and information** – making comparisons between the sounds made by a fire alarm, a bicycle bell and a telephone
- the wide range of **everyday sounds and settings** in which they are heard; for example, doors closing and opening, water running from a tap, car engine and animal sounds
- musical instruments which are specific to **certain cultures**, such as sitar, balalaika and castanets
- **quiet and noisy times of day** and the sounds which can be heard

Safety

Ensure that the children:

- do not put objects in their ears
- take care when handling materials such as sand, peas or marbles, as accidental spillage may cause falls

In the Classroom

Investigations
I wonder whether...

- **some sounds are clearer to hear than others?**

Children can **listen carefully** to a number of sounds, distinguishing which are easy to hear and which are not easy to hear.

By moving the sound source or the listener they could collect information on what difference the distance between the sound and the listener makes, and on whether everyone can hear the same sounds clearly.

- **one instrument can make many sounds?**

Children can **find out** how many sounds they can get from

one musical instrument. For example, they could strike a drum-skin hard or softly, tap it with their finger-tips and finger-nails, and strike it.

They could **compare** these sounds with the sounds that the side of the drum can produce.

- **the volume of the sound can be changed?**

Children can change the contents of containers, or change the size of a container, to alter the volume or pitch of a sound.

They could **compare** the volume of sound when more or less objects are added to the same container, and when a metal container is used instead of a cardboard one.

They could also **compare** the sounds produced on a tambour or chime bar by tapping and beating.

- **sounds are clearer when we are blindfolded?**

Children can begin **identifying** sounds by using the sense of sight as well as hearing.

To find out whether it helps if they can see the sound being made, they can **experiment** wearing a blindfold.

In the Classroom

They can try to identify a sound being made, and to tell from which direction it is coming and how far away it is being made.

What happens if . . .

- **an object is dropped onto different surfaces?**

Children can drop an object such as a coin onto different surfaces; for example carpet, lino, ceramic tile or wooden block. They can **compare** the sounds made, and **gather information** about which materials absorb sound.

They could also **experiment** with dropping the object from different heights, and comparing the sounds made.

- an object is shaken, scraped, tapped or blown into?

Children can **find out** about the range of different sounds an object can make.

Everyday household objects, such as a cup and saucer or a saucepan, or a selection of containers found in the classroom can be used to help children **explore** sounds and **link** their actions with the quality of sound produced.

Can we find a way to . . .

- **change the sounds made by plucking an instrument?**

Children can **look** at the strings on a guitar and **listen** to the sounds the strings produce when plucked. They can compare the effects of shortening the strings and altering the tension.

Children could also alter the size of an elastic band stretched across an empty container. They could **experiment** to find which elastic band makes the lowest sound, and which makes the highest sound.

Different sizes of container could also be used.

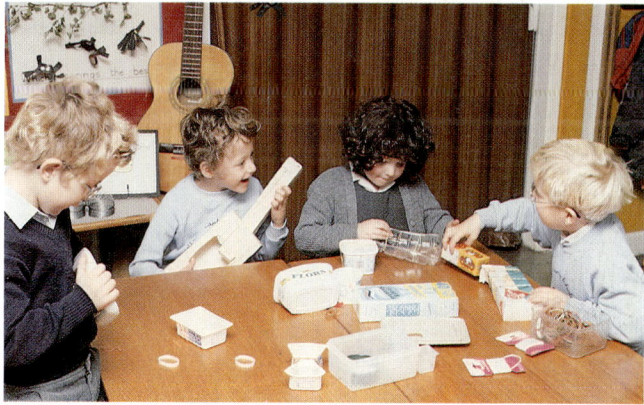

- **make a shaker as a musical instrument?**

35

In the Classroom

Children can **sort** peas, rice, lentils, leaves or paperclips into different closed containers. They can **experiment** with the number of objects needed in each container, and the number of different sounds that can be made.

They could also **compare** the sounds the same objects make in different types and sizes of container.

- **make up a simple tune?**

Children can **collect** a number of empty bottles and listen to the sounds produced when they are blown over or tapped. They can **explore** the changes in sound when they put water in each bottle, and **measure** how much water is needed in each one. They can use different amounts of water to make high and low sounds.

They could also **sort** the sounds in various ways; for example, by pitch or by volume.

- **make sounds quieter?**

Children can **investigate** how well they can hear sounds through a window, a brick wall, a door.

They could experiment with different materials and fabrics; for example, trying to make the sound from a shaker quieter, or to use paper, card, wood or polystyrene to soften the sounds objects make.

Evaluation Checklist

Unit . . . .   Date . . . .

Teaching

Have the children been provided with opportunities to:

- work on questions or problems which they have accepted as their own? ☐

AT14
- work on questions or problems which have enable them to:
  - listen to a variety of sounds? ☐
  - explore and investigate how and when sounds are heard? ☐
- explore and investigate how sounds are produced in simple musical instruments? ☐
  - listen to the sounds produced by different materials? ☐
  - carry out investigations into how sounds are made by using different materials? ☐
  - talk about how sound can travel through the material? ☐

Has the work pupils were engaged in allowed them to:

AT1 • talk about the purposes of recording results? ☐
AT1 • record results by drawing pictures, drawing block graphs and completing frequency charts? ☐
AT1 • sort and group objects and events, such as:
  - musical instruments for a number of different criteria? ☐
  - sounds that we can hear inside the classroom and sounds we cannot hear inside the classroom ☐
AT1 • measure using non-standard and simple standard measuring skill; for example, how far away we can stand and still hear a clock ticking? ☐
AT1 • distinguish between a fair and an unfair test? ☐
AT1 • interpret findings by linking variables? ☐
AT1 • describe activities carried out by sequencing the major features? ☐
AT1 • discuss their observations and ideas with other children? ☐
AT1 • describe the best way of recording their activities? ☐
AT1 • relate their findings to previous ideas and experiences? ☐
AT1 • reflect upon how their procedures might be improved? ☐

Learning

Have the children demonstrated that they can:

Level 1
AT14 • tell you about some of the ways in which sounds can be made? ☐
AT1 • make observations, using their senses, and talk about their observations? ☐

Level 2
AT14 • tell you about when sounds can be heard? ☐
AT14 • talk to you about how musical sounds are produced in simple musical instruments? ☐
AT1 • identify simple variables such as soft/loud, high/low, quiet/loud, dull/ringing, full/empty? ☐
AT1 • ask questions and suggest ideas of the how and why variety? ☐
AT1 • measure using non-standard and standard units? ☐
AT1 • record findings in charts and drawings? ☐
AT1 • list and collate observations? ☐
AT1 • interpret findings by associating one factor with another, such as the distance from a sound affecting how loudly we hear it? ☐

Level 3
AT14 • talk to you about how vibrating objects produce sound? ☐
AT14 • talk to you about sounds and materials and tell you that sound can travel through different materials? ☐
AT14 • tell you how sound is produced in an instrument or object and how it can travel through different materials? ☐
AT1 • formulate hypotheses? ☐
AT1 • distinguish between a fair and an unfair test? ☐
AT1 • identify and describe simple variables that change over time, such as the length of a note? ☐
AT1 • measure using simple measuring instruments, such as a ruler, to the nearest labelled division? ☐
AT1 • record findings in tables and bar charts? ☐
AT1 • describe activities carried out by sequencing the major features? ☐
AT1 • interpret findings in terms of a generalised statement, such as, 'the greater the stretch on an elastic band the higher the note produced'? ☐

© Bishop Grosseteste College 1990. Copying permitted for purchasing school only. This material is not 'copyright free'.

BATTERIES, BUZZERS AND BULBS

UNIT 3
HOW TO MAKE BULBS LIGHT AND BUZZERS SOUND

Opportunities for learning

The range of suggestions in this unit provides children with the following opportunities from the **programme of study** for key stage 1:

- to explore ways of making bulbs and buzzers work
- to investigate which materials will allow electricity to pass through
- to consider the dangers associated with the use of electricity
- to develop their investigative skills and understanding of science in the context of explorations and investigations

The suggestions for practical activities and discussion outlined in this unit provide children with the experiences necessary to facilitate attainment up to level 3.

Topics

Many topics provide children with opportunities for finding out about how to make bulbs light and buzzers sound. Some examples are:

OURSELVES	Surveys about electrical appliances
BUILDINGS	Putting lights on a model Electricity passing through different materials
FESTIVALS	Sources of light Lights on a Christmas tree
FAIRY STORIES SUCH AS 'HANSEL AND GRETEL'	Putting lights in a model house

The flow-diagram in section 1 (figure 3, pp4–5) will help you identify further topics.

Classroom materials

The following Nelson Science materials support this unit:

Picture Resource Book 3

- p.20 – simple, series and parallel circuits
- p.21 – electricity danger-points in the environment
- p.22 – safe use of electricity in the home

Science Discussion Books for key stage 1

- finding out about batteries, buzzers and bulbs

Science Explorers

- **Science Explorer, Carrying Out Surveys 1**
- **Science Explorer, Experimenting 1**
- **Science Explorer, Problem Solving 1**

Planning and Preparation

Related units

Children may ask questions which will provide opportunities for finding out about the content of other units. For example:

- light, shadows, colours and mirrors – unit 1
- using the senses – unit 6
- sounds – unit 2
- everyday materials: sand, wood, metal, plastics, paper, clay, fabrics (including magnets) – unit 20
- using materials to make structures – unit 21

Resources and equipment

- a number of 1.5 V and 3.5 V bulbs
- bulb holders
- small screwdrivers
- buzzers
- wire cutters
- different coloured plastic-covered wire
- 3.5 V batteries
- a selection of materials which can be tested for whether electricity passes through them; for example, metal discs or pieces of metal, string, wool, wood, paper cups, rubber and different coloured wires.

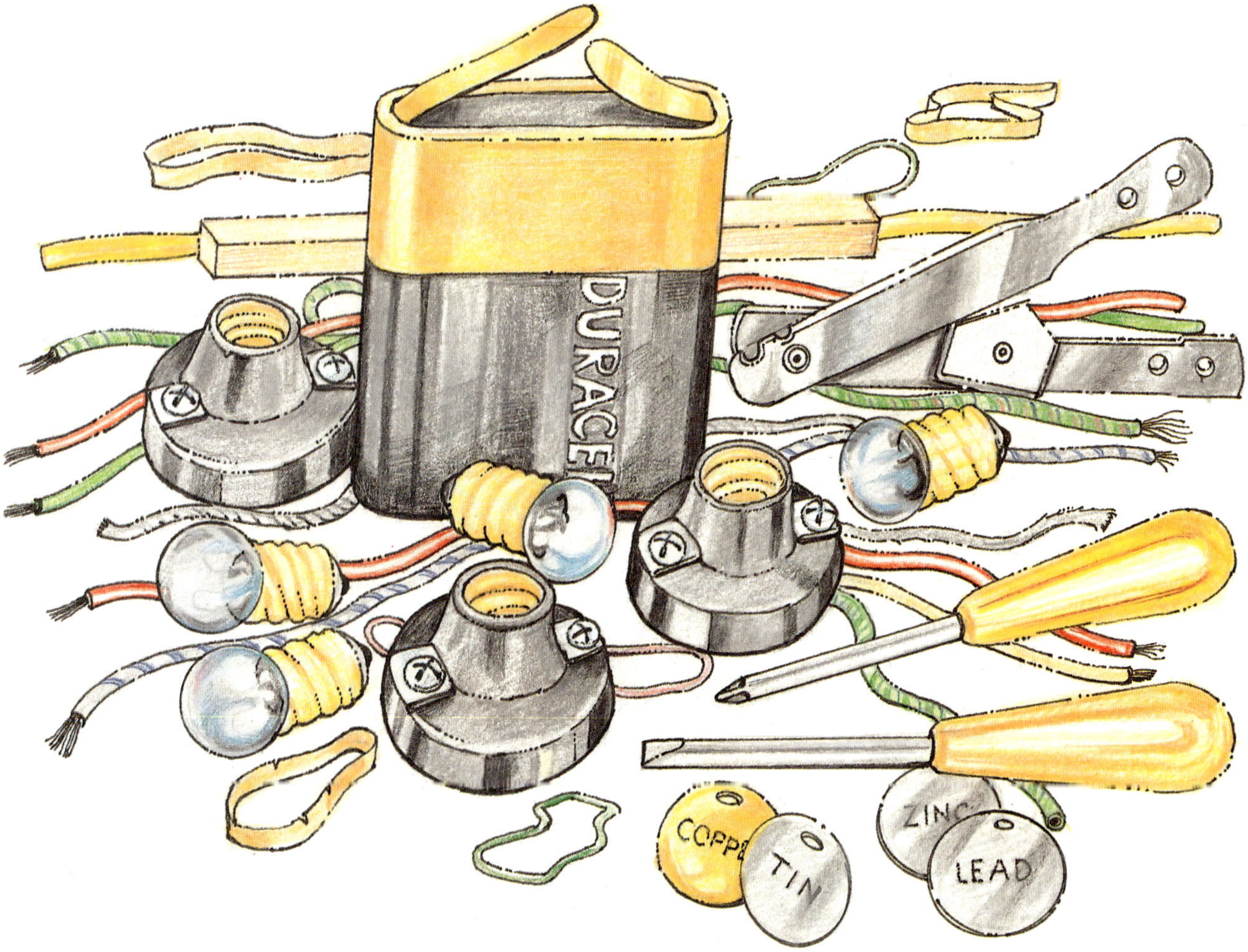

In the Classroom

Getting started
Starting points
Work on how to make bulbs light and buzzers sound can rise from:

children talking about:
- the range of electrical appliances that are found in their homes or at school
- how they can take safe and careful action when handling electrical appliances
- how they can put lights or buzzers onto models they have made
- how a toy such as a torch works

children making collections of:
- torches
- lamps, such as bicycle lamps, miners' lamps and camping lamps
- a number of different light bulbs

children making models such as:
- a house
- a lighthouse
- a vehicle

Asking questions
The activities outlined above could lead to questions such as:

I wonder whether . . .
- we can make the bulbs brighter?
- we can change the sound made by a buzzer?
- a bulb or buzzer will work if different materials are put in a circuit?

What happens if . . .
- we change the colour of the wires used in a circuit?
- we change the length of wires used in a circuit?
- we use double wire in a circuit?
- the battery is turned round?

Can we find a way to . . .
- make a bulb or buzzer work using a battery and wire?

Gathering information
Encourage children to think of ways of **gathering information** to help answer these questions. Investigations which might follow these questions are outlined on pp. 42–44.
Ideas for taking these investigations further are given below.

Further investigations

Carrying out surveys
Collecting information about:
- how a light bulb works
– make a bulb go on and off by making a simple switch
- how batteries work in a circuit
– add more batteries – what happens?
– turn the batteries round – what happens?
- materials which allow electricity to pass through
– make a simple circuit with a bulb, and leave a gap in the circuit
– investigate which materials can be used to bridge the gap and make the bulb light
– sort and group the materials which conduct electricity and those which do not

Experimenting
- making circuits and changing the wire
– use different coloured wires in a circuit, to see if it makes a difference
– change the length of the wire used in a circuit – what happens?

Solving practical problems
- lighting the bulbs on a Christmas tree
– make a circuit and get the Christmas tree lights to work
- Devising a burglar alarm for a model

Handling information
Recording findings
Encourage the children to think about ways in which their findings can be recorded.

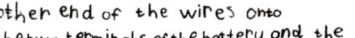

we have a bulb holder and a bulb and put the bulb into the bulb holder. and we had a Battery and two pieces of wire and we wrapped the wire round the screws on the bulb holder we unscrewed the screws and we put the wire a round the screws and screwed the screws back back down we put the other end of the wires onto the two terminals of the battery and the light come on.

In the Classroom

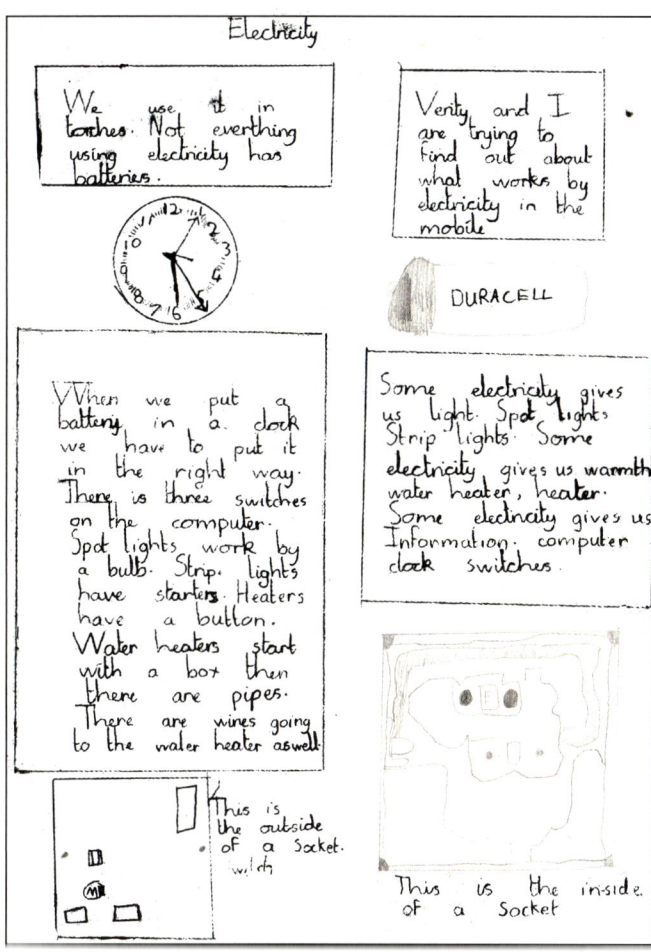

Talk with the children about your reasons for choosing a particular method of recording.

Findings from practical problem-solving activities can be recorded through drawing and writing.

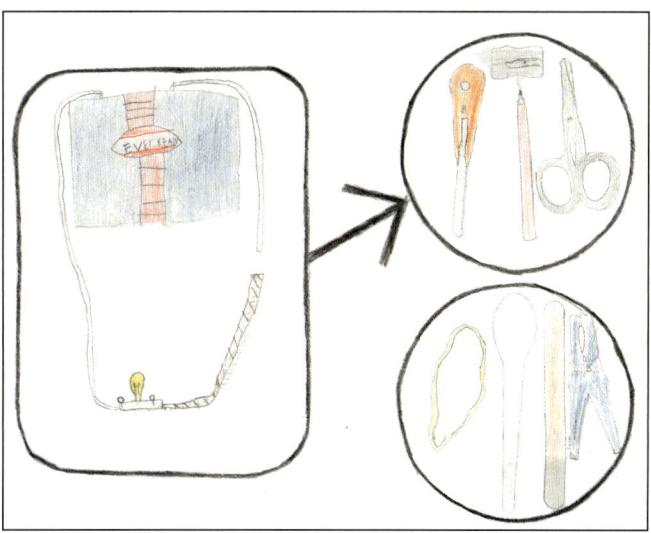

Findings from surveys and experiments can be recorded individually or as a group by:
- using simple charts and pictograms
- using tables and bar charts

Interpreting findings

Encourage children to link findings and observations, and thus try to establish and express cause-and-effect relationships.

Help children to understand that the flow of electricity is from a battery, through the wires to the bulb and round back to the battery.

Review points

The following are useful talking points:

Our investigations
- the questions we asked
- how we planned
- how we collected information
- how and why we recorded
- what we found out

Making connections
- the **range of uses** for electricity in the home, school, shops and factories and how safety is considered; for example, safety switches in the bathroom, protective clothes and footwear in factories
- the **dangers** of playing with electrical equipment and switches
- the **dangers** of playing near pylons, overhead cables and electricity substations

Safety

Ensure that the children:
- are shown the correct way to use wire cutters and screwdrivers
- use only low voltage supplies, such as torch batteries. (N.B. Some local authorities do not permit the use of rechargeable batteries).
- do not use mains electricity during their investigation
- know that electricity and water do not mix

In the Classroom

Investigations
I wonder whether...

- **we can make the bulbs brighter?**

By changing components in a simple circuit children can **collect information** about what makes a bulb light.

Children can add more batteries or a more powerful battery to the circuit.

They could compare the brightness of one bulb and two bulbs in a circuit when only one battery is used.

- **we can change the sound made by a buzzer?**

This investigation is similar to the one above: children can change one component at a time in a circuit in an effort to change the sound made by a buzzer.

What happens if...
- we change the colour of the wires used in a circuit?
- we change the length of wires used in a circuit?
- we use double wire in a circuit?
- the battery is turned round?

This group of questions gives the children an opportunity to find out about how a circuit works.

- **a bulb or buzzer will work if different materials are put in a circuit?**

Children can begin by making a simple circuit with battery, wire and a bulb or buzzer. They can make a gap in the circuit and then compare the effects of using various materials to bridge the gap, by such as a paperclip, a matchstick, a pencil or a crayon, to try to make the bulbs light or the buzzer work again.

In the Classroom

Children can be given a number of different coloured wires of different lengths. They can **investigate** whether changing the colour or length of wires, or using two strands twisted together, makes a difference to the brightness of the bulbs or the sound made by the buzzer.

They can also investigate whether the bulb will light or the buzzer work if the battery is turned round.

Can we find a way to . . .

- **make a bulb or buzzer work using a battery and wire?**

In the Classroom

Early **exploration** is important. Help the children to find out how to make a complete circuit.

Talk about and draw what they have done.

Evaluation Checklist

Unit .... Date ....

Teaching
Have the children been provided with opportunities to:

- Work on questions or problems which they have accepted as their own? ☐

AT11
- Work on questions or problems which have enabled them to:
    - Observe and talk about a wide range of household electrical appliances, and how to use them safely? ☐
    - Become aware of the dangers associated with using mains electricity? ☐
    - Explore and investigate a wide range of objects and materials to see if electricity will pass through them? ☐
    - Carry out investigations with batteries, bulbs and wires to find how to make a bulb work? ☐
    - Carry out investigations with batteries, buzzers and wires to find how to make a buzzer work? ☐

Has the work pupils were engaged in allowed them to:

AT1 • talk about the purposes of recording results? ☐

AT1 • record results by drawing pictures, drawing block graphs and completing frequency charts, table and bar charts? ☐

AT1 • sort and group objects and events, such as:
- materials which allow electricity to pass through and those which do not? ☐

AT1 • distinguish between a fair and an unfair test? ☐

AT1 • interpret findings by linking variables? ☐

AT1 • describe activities carried out by sequencing the major features? ☐

AT1 • discuss their observations and ideas with other children? ☐

AT1 • describe the best way of recording their activities? ☐

AT1 • relate their findings to previous ideas and experiences? ☐

AT1 • reflect upon how their procedures might be improved? ☐

Learning
Have the children demonstrated that they can:

Level 1
AT11 • tell you about household appliances that use electricity? ☐

AT11 • give some examples of the dangerous misuse of electrical appliances? ☐

AT1 • make observations using all their senses and talk about their observations? ☐

Level 2
AT11 • give an account of some of the dangers associated with the use of mains electricity? ☐

AT11 • give some examples of how to use electricity safely? ☐

AT1 • ask questions and suggest ideas of the how and why variety? ☐

AT1 • record findings in charts and drawings ☐

AT1 • list and collate observations? ☐

AT1 • interpret findings by associating one factor with another, such as the need for a complete circuit to make a bulb or buzzer work? ☐

Level 3
AT11 • give some examples of materials which conduct electricity well and some examples of materials which do not conduct electricity well? ☐

AT11 • construct a complete circuit using a battery, wires and either a bulb or a buzzer? ☐

AT11 • talk to you about the flow of electricity from the battery, through the wire to the bulb or buzzer and round back to the battery again? ☐

AT1 • formulate hypotheses? ☐

AT1 • distinguish between a fair and an unfair test? ☐

AT1 • record findings in tables and bar charts? ☐

AT1 • interpret simple pictograms and bar charts? ☐

AT1 • describe activities carried out by sequencing the major features? ☐

AT1 • interpret findings in terms of a generalised statement, such as 'the greater the number of batteries in a circuit the brighter the light'? ☐

© Bishop Grosseteste College 1990. Copying permitted for purchasing school only. This material is not 'copyright free'.

HOW PEOPLE CHANGE THE ENVIRONMENT

UNIT 4
IMPROVING THE APPEARANCE OF THE LOCAL ENVIRONMENT

Opportunities for learning

The range of suggestions in this unit provides children with the following opportunities from the **programme of study** for key stage 1:

- to investigate the extent to which everyday waste products decay naturally
- to record their observations and use this knowledge to help improve the appearance of the local environment
- to develop their investigative skills and understanding of science in the context of explorations and investigations

The suggestions for practical activities and discussion outlined in this unit provide children with the experiences necessary to facilitate attainment up to level 3.

Topics

Many topics provide children with opportunities for finding out about improving the appearance of the local environment. Some examples are:

WEATHER	Effect of the weather on materials How materials rot
FOOD	Food that is thrown away Packaging of food
CHANGE	Growth and decay of plants
SHOPPING	Different types of container and packaging
RUBBISH	Litter control Keeping the environment tidy
OURSELVES	The food we eat
THE PARK	Keeping the local park tidy Investigations into litter control

The flow-diagram in section 1 (figure 3, pp.4–5) will help you identify further topics.

Classroom materials

The following Nelson Science materials support this unit:

Picture Resource Book 2

- p.19 – effects of oil pollution on animal life
- p.20 – conservation of the environment
- p.21 – decay of waste products
- p.22 – bar chart of periods of decay

Planning and Preparation

Science Discussion Books for key stage 1
- finding out about how people change the environment

Science Explorers
- **Science Explorer, Carrying Out Surveys 1**
- **Science Explorer, Experimenting 1**
- **Science Explorer, Problem Solving 1**

Related units
Children may ask questions which will provide opportunities for finding out about the content of other units. For example:

– feeding – unit 7
– seasonal and daily changes in plants — unit 13
– natural materials found in the locality: stones, rocks, soil – unit 18
– everyday materials: sand, wood, metal, plastics, paper, clay, fabrics (including magnets) – unit 20

Resources and equipment
- soil and/or compost
- rubber gloves
- a hand lens or microscope
- tweezers
- inspection containers
- bags and other containers such as yogurt pots and plastic trays
- leaf litter
- a selection of packages and containers made from different materials, such as paper, card, plastic and metal
- a wormery

In the Classroom

Getting started

Starting points
Work on improving the appearance of the local environment can arise from:

children talking about:
- the food they eat and how they dispose of left-over food
- the different packages that contain food
- seasonal changes in trees
- litter blowing around in the playground
- the work of the refuse collectors
- jobs done by the caretaker

children making collections of:
- clean rubbish collected over several days
- different packages and containers
- different materials both natural, such as shells, stones, leaves etc., and manufactured, such as different types of plastic

children visiting:
- a building site
- a park
- a farm

Asking Questions
The activities outlined above could lead to questions such as:

I wonder whether . . .
- some materials rot or decay faster than others?
- the bottom layers of leaf litter are the same as the top layers?

What happens if . . .
- different waste products are covered with sand or soil?
- food, such as bread or biscuits, is kept in different conditions?
- leaves, or other vegetation, are kept in different conditions?
- leaves, or other vegetation, are put onto the surface of a wormery?

Can we find a way to . . .
- stop litter blowing around the playground?
- recycle or re-use materials?

Gathering information
Encourage children to think of ways of **gathering information** to help answer these questions.

Investigations which might follow these questions are outlined on pp. 50–52.

Ideas for taking these investigations further are given below.

Further investigations

Carrying out surveys
Collecting information about:
- the types of thing thrown out during a day
  - observe, sort and group these things
  - observe what happens over a period of time to waste material placed in the environment
- natural and manufactured things in the environment
  - observe, sort and group the things in the environment which are natural and manufactured
  - observe, sort and group the things that are useful to the environment, and those that are harmful
- making improvements to the immediate environment
  - investigate encouraging the growth of plants
  - explore how to attract wild life
  - investigate keeping the immediate environment tidy

Experimenting
- testing the effects of water or temperature on waste products
  - use a variety of different materials
  - compare the changes
  - observe what happens to the water

Solving practical problems
- creating and maintaining a litter-free playground
- encouraging the growth of wild plants and animals in the environment

Handling information

Recording findings
Encourage the children to think about ways in which their findings can be recorded.

Talk with the children about your reasons for choosing a particular method of recording.

In the Classroom

Findings from practical problem-solving activities can be recorded through drawing and writing.

Findings from surveys and experiments can be recorded individually or as a group by:

- using simple charts and pictograms
- using tables and bar charts

Thursday — Its going browner. Its soft and squashy.

Friday — still no mould.

Monday — Its got some mould. It is soft on the outside.

Tuesday — No more mould than yesterday.

Wednesday — Its got more mould

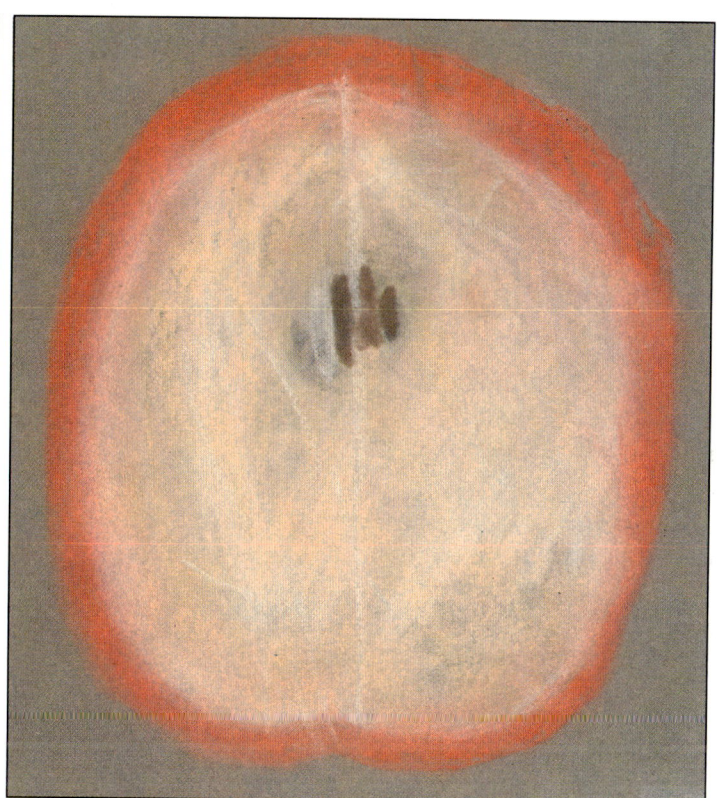

We have been thinking about keeping our school tidy	
The contents of the waste bin	
What we found	**How many we found**
Crisp packets	x x x x x x x x
Apple cores	x x x
Sweet wrappers	x x x x x x
Scrap paper	x x

49

In the Classroom

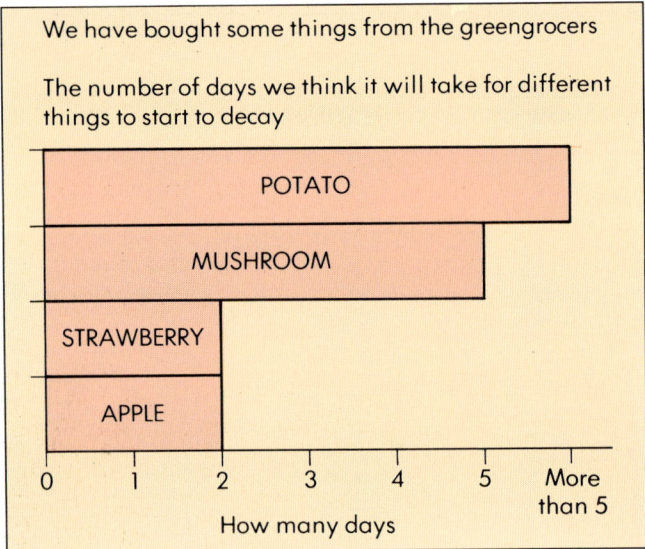

We have bought some things from the greengrocers

The number of days we think it will take for different things to start to decay

Interpreting findings
Encourage children to link findings and observations, and thus try to establish and express cause-and effect relationships.

Help children to understand that some waste products decay naturally but do so over different periods of time.

Review points
The following are useful talking points:

Our investigations
- the questions we asked
- how we planned
- how we collected information
- how and why we recorded
- what we found out

Making connections
- the **differences** between everyday waste products that occur **naturally** such as trees losing their leaves, and those that **people create**, such as bottles and cans
- the materials that can be **recycled** and re-used, such as glass and paper
- what happens to the waste collected by the **refuse collectors** – disposal techniques such as tipping, pulverisation and incineration
- ways in which people could **help to improve** the appearance of their local environment

Safety
Ensure that the children:
- do not handle glass
- wash their hands thoroughly after handling rubbish or soil
- carefully destroy any moulds which have been grown

Investigations

I wonder whether . . .
- **some materials rot or decay faster than others**

Children will probably begin to appreciate the process of decay by noticing that the flowers brought into the classroom on Monday morning are beginning to die by Friday.

They can **make comparisons** between other plants – for example, fresh grass cuttings or soft, fresh fruit – by **observing** the changes that occur over a number of days.

Examples of litter could be **collected** and **sorted**, and children could observe what happens to them over time.

- **the bottom layers of leaf litter are the same as the top layers?**

Children can **make observations** of the content of leaf litter and of the changes that occur – over a longer period of time.

They could also **investigate** the evidence of how natural 'decomposers', such as worms, help in the process.

In the Classroom

What happens if . . .

- **different waste products are covered with sand or soil?**

The children can **select** a range of different waste products, such as an apple core, a crisp packet, a piece of newspaper, and a lollipop stick, and cover them with the selected medium.

They can **identify and control** some of the variables which might affect the result, such as the amount of sand or soil used to cover the object, whether the sand or soil is wet or dry, and the length of time for which the object will be left covered.

- **food, such as bread or biscuits, is kept in different conditions?**

Children can **compare** the changes that occur to food kept in dry or damp conditions, covering the food or leaving it exposed.

The children could **collect information** about how decay or waste can be prevented or slowed down.

- **leaves, or other vegetation, are kept in different conditions?**

The children could carry out similar **investigations** to those outlined above, but use garden refuse instead of food.

- **leaves, or other vegetation, are put onto the surface of a wormery?**

After setting up a wormery, children can **observe** how worms help in the decomposition of material.

In the Classroom

They could **sort** the types of vegetation they put onto the **surface**, and record how long it takes for the worms to pull the vegetation down into the soil.

Can we find a way to . . .

- **stop litter blowing around the playground?**

The children can design and make a rubbish bin. They can experiment to find the best size, shape and material used in the construction, and the best position for the rubbish bin.

- **recycle or re-use materials?**

Children can make paper from other materials, such as egg cartons or newspaper.

They could also re-use cartons in box modelling.

Evaluation Checklist

Unit .... Date ....

Teaching

Have the children been provided with opportunities to:

- work on questions or problems which they have accepted as their own? ☐
- AT5 work on questions or problems which have enabled them to:
  - explore and investigate the extent to which everyday waste products decay naturally? ☐
  - help to improve the appearance of their local environment? ☐

Has the work pupils were engaged in allowed them to:

- AT1 • talk about the purposes of recording results? ☐
- AT1 • record results by drawing pictures, drawing block graphs and completing frequency charts, tables and bar charts? ☐
- AT1 • sort and group objects, such as:
  - a selection of everyday waste products produced naturally? ☐
  - a selection of everyday waste products produced by human activity? ☐
- AT1 • measure using non-standard and simple standard measuring skills; for example, how long it takes for daisies in a vase of water to die? ☐
- AT1 • distinguish between a fair and an unfair test? ☐
- AT1 • interpret findings by linking variables? ☐
- AT1 • describe activities carried out by sequencing the major features? ☐
- AT1 • discuss their observations and ideas with other children? ☐
- AT1 • describe the best way of recording their activities? ☐
- AT1 • relate their findings to previous ideas and experiences? ☐
- AT1 • reflect upon how their procedures might be improved? ☐
- AT1 • work in a safe and careful manner? ☐

Learning

Have the children demonstrated that they can:

Level 1

- AT5 • give some examples of the waste products produced by human activity? ☐
- AT1 • make observations about some of the waste materials and talk about their observations? ☐

Level 2

- AT5 • talk to you about how some waste products decay? ☐
- AT5 • keep a diary about change that occurs over time? ☐
- AT1 • identify simple variables such as wet/dry, clean/dirty, hot/cold? ☐
- AT1 • ask questions and suggest ideas of the 'how' and 'why' variety? ☐
- AT1 • measure using non-standard and standard units? ☐
- AT1 • record findings in charts and drawings? ☐
- AT1 • list and collate observations? ☐
- AT1 • interpret findings by associating one factor with another, such as exposure to air affecting the freshness of food? ☐

Level 3

- AT5 • tell you about some of the human activities which may produce changes in the air, water and land of the local environment; for example, discharge from factories, bonfires in the garden, tipping rubbish? ☐
- AT1 • give an account of a project to help improve the local environment? ☐
- AT1 • formulate hypotheses? ☐
- AT1 • distinguish between a fair and an unfair test? ☐
- AT1 • measure using simple measuring instruments, such as a ruler, to the nearest labelled division? ☐
- AT1 • record findings in tables and bar charts? ☐
- AT1 • describe activities carried out by sequencing the major features? ☐
- AT1 • interpret findings in terms of a generalised statement, such as 'some waste products decay naturally, but often do so over a long period of time'? ☐
- AT1 • work in a safe and careful way? ☐

© Bishop Grosseteste College 1990. Copying permitted for purchasing school only. This material is not 'copyright free'.

THEMSELVES AND OTHERS AND HOW TO KEEP HEALTHY

UNIT 5
GROWING AND MOVING

Opportunities for learning

The range of suggestions in this unit provides children with the following opportunities from the **programme of study** for key stage 1:

- to find out about how they grow and move
- to consider how they keep healthy through exercise, personal safety and the safe use of medicines
- to explore ways in which they and other children are similar and different
- to develop their investigative skills and understanding of science in the context of explorations and investigations

The suggestions for practical activities and discussion outlined in this unit provide children with the experiences necessary to facilitate attainment up to level 3.

Topics

Many topics provide children with opportunities for finding out about growing and moving. Some examples are:

OURSELVES	Themselves and younger and older human beings Products designed to wash and clean Food that they eat Effects of exercise and rest Caring for teeth Similarities and differences
CHANGE	Similarities and differences Themselves and younger and older human beings
WATER	Products designed to wash and clean How to keep clean
MOVEMENT	How we move The effects of exercise and rest
FOOD	Food that they eat

The flow-diagram in section 1 (figure 3, pp.4–5) will help you identify further topics.

Classroom Materials

The following Nelson Science materials support this unit:

Picture Resource Book 2

- p.1 – changing with age
- p.2 – growth at different ages
- p.3 – parts of the body

Planning and Preparation

Science Discussion Books for key stage 1
- finding out about themselves and others and how to keep healthy

Science Explorers
- **Science Explorer, Carrying Out Surveys 1**
- **Science Explorer, Experimenting 1**

Other useful materials from Nelson are:
- **Health for Life 1**
- **Health for Life 2**

Related units

Children may ask questions which will provide opportunities for finding out about the content of other units. For example:

- feeding – Unit 7
- how to take care of plants – Unit 8
- how plant life varies – Unit 9
- how to take care of animals – Unit 11
- how animal life varies – Unit 12
- how to make things move – Unit 17

Resources and equipment

- standard and non-standard measuring units
- pictures and photographs of babies, children and adults
- different soaps and soap powders

In the Classroom

Getting started

Starting points
Work on growing and moving can arise from:

children talking about:
- a new skill they have mastered, such as swimming or skipping
- similarities and differences they have noticed in other children
- their new shoes or clothes

Children visiting or having visits
- from a new baby brother or sister
- from the school nurse
- to a dentist
- to a doctor or hospital

children taking part in school events such as:
- sports day
- medical examinations

children making collections of:
- different sizes of clothes or shoes

children reading/listening to stories such as:
- 'Tom Thumb'
- 'The Tiny Seed and the Giant Flower'
- 'Thumbelina'
- 'Peter Pan'

Asking questions
The activities outlined above could lead to questions such as:

> **I wonder whether . . .**
> - every child in the class is the same height?
> - every child in the class has the same sized feet?
> - every child in the class has the same sized hands?
> - every child in the class has the same number of teeth?
> - the tallest child in the class has the largest feet/ biggest hands/biggest head circumference:
> - the tallest child in the class is the oldest?
> - every child in the class can:
> – skip with a skipping rope?
> – swim?
> – ride a bicycle?

> **What happens if . . .**
> - we walk around the playground?
> - we run around the playground?
> - we wash our dirty hands in:
> – cold water?
> – warm water?
> – cold/warm water with soap?

Gathering information
Encourage children to think of ways of gathering information to help answer these questions.

Investigations which might follow these questions are outlined on pp.58–60.

Ideas for taking these investigations further are given below.

Further investigations

> **Carrying out surveys**
> **Collecting information about:**
> - how many different ways people move
> – observe which parts of their bodies they use when they run/jump/skip/swim
> - how people change as they get older
> – compare the way a baby moves with the way elderly people move
> – observe the changes that happen to people's bodies as they get older
> - things that keep us healthy
> – sort and group the things which help to keep people healthy

Handling information

Recording findings
Encourage the children to think about ways in which their findings can be recorded.

Talk with the children about your reasons for choosing a particular method of recording.

Findings from practical problem-solving activities can be recorded through drawing and writing.

Findings from surveys and experiments can be recorded individually or as a group by:
- using simple charts and pictograms

In the Classroom

- using tables and bar charts

Children in my group who can do these things			
Sabera			
David	David		
Helen	Helen		
Aziz	Emily	Sabera	David
Paul	Famita	Paul	Hasan
Skip with a rope	Swim	Roller skate	Skate board

In the Classroom

Interpreting findings
Encourage children to link findings and observations, and thus try to establish cause-and-effect relationships.

Help children to link exercise and movement with an increased rate in breathing.

Review points
The following are useful talking points:

Our investigations
- the questions we asked
- how we planned
- how we collected information
- how and why we recorded
- what we found out

Making connections
- children's ideas about the ways in which **the young of several species** are born
- children's ideas about how **babies** are born
- what happens to the human body when it is **resting**
- skills which develop with **age and maturity**; for example, crawling, walking, swimming, gymnastics, writing, sewing
- people with **disabilities**
- the names of the external **parts of the human body**
- the safe and careful use and storage of **medicines**

Safety
Ensure that the children:
- are fit and well enough to take part in strenuous physical exercise

Investigations

I wonder whether . . .
- every child in the class is the same height?

- every child in the class has the same sized feet?
- every child in the class has the same sized hands?

- every child in the class has the same number of teeth?

In the Classroom

By **observing and recording** these simple differences between each other, children can **collect information** about how living things vary from one individual to the next.

- the tallest child in the class has the largest feet/ biggest hands/biggest head circumference?
- the tallest child in the class is the heaviest?
- the tallest child in the class is the oldest?

Children can begin to **use the information** that they have **collected** to help them understand that human beings grow and develop at different rates.

- every child in the class can:
– skip with a skipping rope?

– swim?
– ride a bicycle?

Children can begin to **link** their movements with certain skills which they are developing.

What happens if . . .
- we walk around the playground?
- we run around the playground?

Children can **feel** their heart beating or feel their pulse in their wrist or neck before and after the exercise.

Their attention might be drawn to their rate of breathing and to whether or not their skin feels hot.

59

In the Classroom

- **we wash dirty hands in – cold water? – warm water? – cold/warm water with soap?**

By trying to find the best way to wash dirty hands children can begin to **realise the importance** of simple washing routines in personal hygiene.

Evaluation Checklist

Unit . . . .   Date . . . .

Teaching

Have the children been provided with opportunities to:

- work on questions or problems which they have accepted as their own? ☐

AT3
- work on questions or problems which have enabled them to:
  - explore ways in which they move? ☐
  - talk about and investigate similarities and differences between themselves and younger and older human beings? ☐
  - talk about ways of keeping safe and well? ☐
  - talk about their body? ☐

AT4
- explore and talk about the ways in which living things vary from one individual to another? ☐

Has the work pupils were engaged in allowed them to:

AT1 • talk about the purposes of recording results? ☐
AT1 • record results by drawing pictures, drawing block graphs and completing frequency charts, tables and bar charts? ☐
AT1 • sort and group objects and events, such as;
  - children who have brown hair and those who do not? ☐
  - children who can swim and those who cannot? ☐
AT1 • measure using non-standard and simple standard measuring skills; for example, a child's height in hand-spans? ☐
AT1 • distinguish between a fair and an unfair test? ☐
AT1 • interpret findings by linking variables? ☐
AT1 • describe activities carried out by sequencing the major features? ☐
AT1 • discuss their observations and ideas with other children? ☐
AT1 • describe the best way of recording their activities? ☐
AT1 • relate their findings to previous ideas and experiences? ☐
AT1 • reflect upon how their procedures might be improved? ☐

Learning

Have the children demonstrated that they can:

Level 1
AT3 • tell you the external parts of the human body e.g. arm, leg, head, foot, hand? ☐
AT4 • tell you about some of the differences between individual human beings? ☐
AT1 • make observations about themselves and talk about their observations? ☐

Level 2
AT3 • talk to you about babies being the young of human beings? ☐
AT3 • give some examples of ways in which they can keep clean? ☐
AT3 • talk to you about the food that they eat? ☐
AT3 • tell you about ways in which they take exercise and rest? ☐
AT3 • talk about some of the safe and careful actions they can take? ☐
AT4 • measure, using standard and non-standard units, simple differences between each other: for example, height? ☐
AT1 • identify simple variables such as tall/short, wide/narrow, fast/slow? ☐
AT1 • ask questions and suggest ideas of the 'how' and 'why' variety? ☐
AT1 • record findings in charts and drawings? ☐
AT1 • list and collate observations? ☐
AT1 • interpret findings by associating one factor with another, such as food giving us energy? ☐

Level 3
AT3 • talk to you about the ways in which human beings and other living things breathe and move? ☐
AT3 • describe to you through talking the main stages in the human life cycle i.e. baby, child, adult? ☐
AT1 • formulate hypotheses? ☐
AT1 • identify and describe simple variables that change over time, such as the height and weight of a human being? ☐
AT1 • distinguish between a fair and an unfair test? ☐
AT1 • measure using simple measuring instruments, such as a ruler, to the nearest labelled division? ☐
AT1 • record findings in tables and bar charts? ☐
AT1 • interpret simple pictograms and bar charts? ☐
AT1 • describe activities carried out by sequencing the major features? ☐

© Bishop Grosseteste College 1990. Copying permitted for purchasing school only. This material is not 'copyright free'.

61

THEMSELVES AND OTHERS AND HOW TO KEEP HEALTHY

UNIT 6
USING THE SENSES

Opportunities for learning

The range of suggestions in this unit provides children with the following opportunities from the **programme of study** for key stage 1:

- to explore ways in which they use their senses
- to explore ways in which they and other children are similar and different
- to develop their investigative skills and understanding of science in the context of explorations and investigations

The suggestions for practical activities and discussion outlined in this unit provide children with the experiences necessary to facilitate attainment up to level 3.

Topics

Many topics provide children with opportunities for finding out about using the senses. Some examples are:

OURSELVES	– How they feed – The food that they eat – The sounds they can hear – Using their eyes – Touching and feeling – Similarities and differences
THE SENSES	– How they feed – The sounds they can hear – Touching and feeling
LIGHT AND DARK	– Using their eyes
OUR TOWN	– Sounds they can hear
MATERIALS	– Touching and feeling

The flow-diagram in section 1 (figure 3, pp.4–5) will help you identify further topics.

Classroom materials

The following Nelson Science materials support this unit:

Picture Resource Book 2

- p. 7 – effect of light on the human eye

Science Discussion Books for key stage 1
- finding out about themselves and others and how to keep healthy

Science Explorers
- **Science Explorer, Carrying Out Surveys 1**
- **Science Explorers, Experimenting 1**

Other useful materials from Nelson are:

- **Health for Life 1**
- **Health for Life 2**

Planning and Preparation

Related units
Children may ask questions which will provide opportunities for finding out about the content of other units. For example:

- light, shadows, colours and mirrors – unit 1
- sounds – unit 2
- how to take care of plants – unit 8
- how plant life varies – unit 9
- how to take care of animals – unit 11
- how animal life varies – unit 12
- everyday materials: sand, wood, metal, plastics, paper, clay, fabrics (including magnets) – unit 20

Resources and equipment
- samples of food to taste, such as raw vegetables and fruit; for example, apple, potato, carrot
- a tape-recorder to tape sounds in the environment, household sounds, classroom sounds and warning sounds
- a torch
- a blindfold

In the Classroom

Getting started

Starting points
Work on using the senses can arise from:

children talking about:
- food they like or dislike
- meal times
- the content of their lunch box

children visiting or walking around:
- the school
- a park
- the local streets
- a farm or factory

children reading/listening to stories such as:
- 'Each Peach, Pear, Plum'
- 'The Pied Piper of Hamlin'
- 'After Dark'

Asking questions
The activities outlined above could lead to questions such as:

I wonder whether . . .
- food can be identified by one sense only?
- food tastes the same on each part of the tongue?
- objects can be identified by touch alone?
- we all hear the same things?
- the children in my class have different coloured eyes or hair?

What happens if . . .
- I cover up my ears?
- I put my hand behind my ear?
- I close my eyes and listen?

Gathering information
Encourage children to think of ways of **gathering information** to help answer these questions.
Investigations which might follow these questions are outlined on pp. 66–68.
Ideas for taking these investigations further are given below.

Further investigations

Carrying out surveys
Collecting information about:
- how our senses help us
 – explore how we feel things
 – observe the parts of our hands which are used when we pick up an object
 – touch a variety of things and sort them for a number of different criteria
- how we use our senses
 – investigate how we eat things
 – identify common foods by using the senses
 – collect information about favourite foods
 – collect information about how many meals we eat

Experimenting
- making comparisons between the way we use our senses
 – collect information about individual children when one of their senses is isolated; for example, investigate whether all the children can identify apple by smell, taste or touch alone

Handling information

Recording findings
Encourage the children to think about ways in which their findings can be recorded.

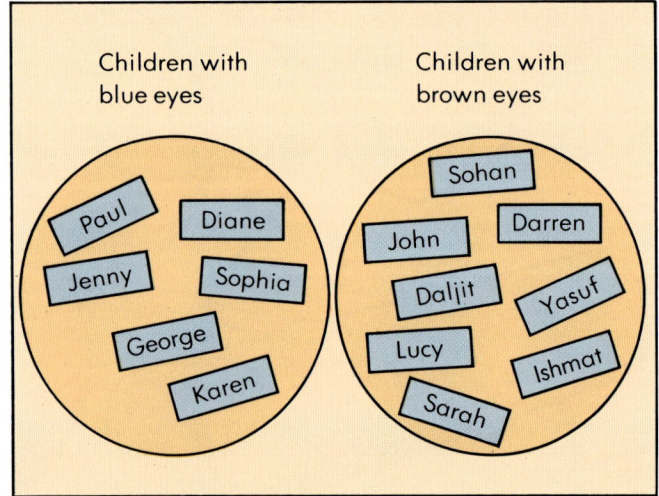

In the Classroom

Talk with the children about your reasons for choosing a particular method of recording.

Findings from practical problem-solving activities can be recorded through drawing and writing.

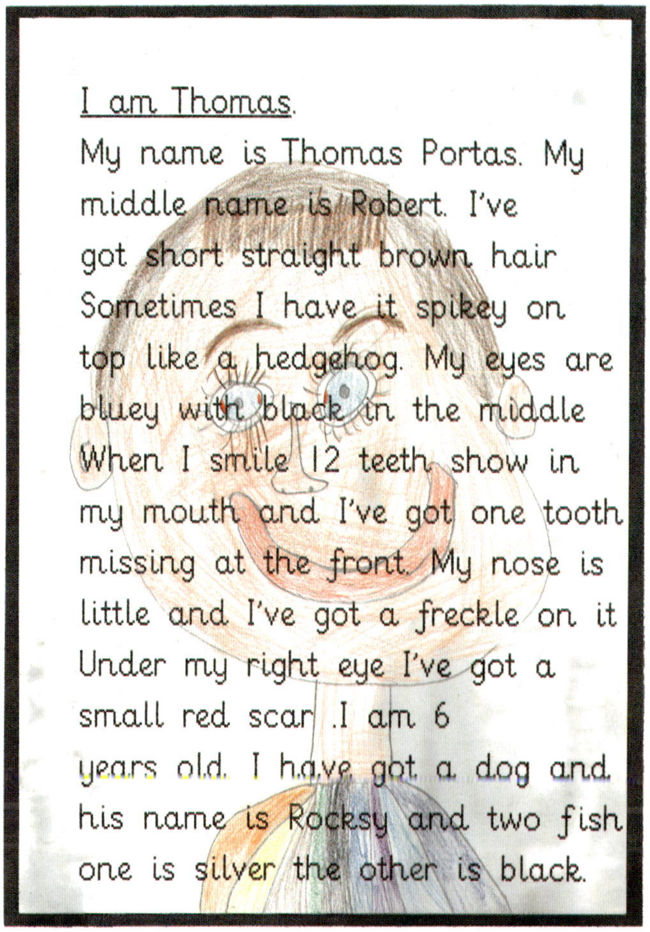

> **I am Thomas.**
> My name is Thomas Portas. My middle name is Robert. I've got short straight brown hair Sometimes I have it spikey on top like a hedgehog. My eyes are bluey with black in the middle When I smile 12 teeth show in my mouth and I've got one tooth missing at the front. My nose is little and I've got a freckle on it Under my right eye I've got a small red scar. I am 6 years old. I have got a dog and his name is Rocksy and two fish one is silver the other is black.

Findings from surveys and experiments can be recorded individually or as a group by:
- using simple charts and pictograms
- using tables and bar charts

Favourite Fruits	
Banana	X X X X X X X X X X
Apple	X X X X
Mango	X X X X X X X X
Tomato	X X X

In the Classroom

Interpreting findings

Encourage children to link findings and observations, and thus try to establish and express cause-and-effect relationships.

Help children to link the changes they make to the effects they observe – for example, if they cover up their ears they can hear less well; if they eliminate the sense of sight they can identify objects less accurately.

Review points

The following are useful talking points:

Our investigations

- the questions we asked
- how we planned
- how we collected information
- how and why we recorded
- what we found out

Making connections

- how they use their senses throughout the pattern of **their own day**
- sounds that are useful such as **warning and information sounds**; for example, car horn, bicycle bell, fire alarm, door bell, telephone
- the names of the **external parts of the human body**
- people with **disabilities**, such as blindness, deafness, other physical disabilities

Safety

Ensure that the children:

- carefully handle any object which is held close to the eye
- are constantly supervised when they are tasting things
- do not push objects into their ears or noses

Investigations

I wonder whether . . .

- **food can be identified by one sense only?**

By isolating one sense, children can try to identify food such as vegetables and fruit by smell only, taste only, touch only

- **food tastes the same on each part of the tongue?**

Sugar and salt can be dissolved in water and then drops of the solution can be placed on different areas of the tongue.

In the Classroom

Children can begin to **find out** about the sensitivity of the tongue.

- **objects can be identified by touch alone?**

Children can handle a variety of objects and try to **identify** them through the sense of touch.

- **we all hear the same things?**

Children can listen to a clock or watch ticking, or listen to a safety pin being dropped on a hard surface, and measure the distances across which different children can hear these things.

In the Classroom

- the children in my class have different coloured eyes or hair?

By **observing and recording** these simple differences between each other the

children can **collect information** about how living things vary from one individual to the next.

What happens if . . .

- I cover up my ears?
- I put my hand behind my ear?
- I close my eyes and listen?

Children can **find out** about how they use their senses by trying these simple experiments. If they cover their ears they will find that sounds are muffled; if they cup their hands behind their ears they might find that sound is enhanced, if they listen carefully while their eyes are closed or blindfolded they might be able to hear quieter sounds over longer distances.

Evaluation Checklist

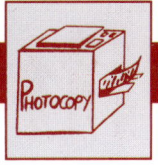

Unit .... Date ....

Teaching

Have the children been provided with opportunities to:

- work on questions or problems which they have accepted as their own? ☐
- work on questions or problems which have enabled them to:

AT3 – Explore and talk about the ways in which they use their senses? ☐

AT4 – Explore and talk about similarities and differences between themselves and other children? ☐

Has the work pupils were engaged in allowed them to:

AT1 • talk about the purposes of recording results? ☐

AT1 • record results by drawing pictures, drawing block graphs and completing frequency charts, tables and bar charts? ☐

AT1 • sort and group objects and events, such as:
- food which tastes sweet and food that does not taste sweet?
- children who have blue eyes and those who do not? ☐

AT1 • measure using non-standard and simple standard measuring skills; for example, how far away we can stand and still hear a pin dropping? ☐

AT1 • distinguish between a fair and an unfair test? ☐

AT1 • interpret findings by linking variables? ☐

AT1 • describe activities carried out by sequencing the major features? ☐

AT1 • discuss their observations and ideas with other children? ☐

AT1 • describe the best way of recording their activities? ☐

AT1 • relate their findings to previous ideas and experiences? ☐

AT1 • reflect upon how their procedures might be improved? ☐

Learning

Have the children demonstrated that they can:

Level 1

AT3 • tell you the external parts of the human body, such as nose, nostrils, eye, pupil, iris, hands, fingers? ☐

AT4 • tell you about some of the differences between individual human beings? ☐

AT1 • make observations using all of their senses and talk about their observations? ☐

Level 2

AT3 • tell you about the pattern and routine of their own day? ☐

AT4 • use standard and non-standard measures to measure simple differences between each other? ☐

AT1 • identify simple variables such as sweet/sour, light/dark, quiet/loud? ☐

AT1 • ask questions and suggest ideas of the 'how' and 'why' variety? ☐

AT1 • record findings in charts and drawings? ☐

AT1 • list and collate observations? ☐

Level 3

AT3 • tell you about the ways in which human beings and other living things use their senses? ☐

AT1 • formulate hypotheses? ☐

AT1 • distinguish between a fair and an unfair test? ☐

AT1 • measure using simple measuring instruments, such as a ruler, to the nearest labelled division? ☐

AT1 • record findings in tables and bar charts? ☐

AT1 • interpret simple pictograms and bar charts? ☐

AT1 • describe activities carried out by sequencing the major features? ☐

© Bishop Grosseteste College 1990. Copying permitted for purchasing school only. This material is not 'copyright free'.

THEMSELVES AND OTHERS AND HOW TO KEEP HEALTHY

UNIT 7
FEEDING

Opportunities for learning

The range of suggestions in this unit provides children with the following opportunities from the programme of study for key stage 1:

- to explore ways in which they can keep healthy through eating
- to explore ways in which they and other children are similar and different
- to explore a range of food, giving consideration to what, why and when they eat
- to develop their investigative skills and understanding of science in the context of explorations and investigations

The suggestions for practical activities and discussion outlined in this unit provide children with the experiences necessary to facilitate attainment up to level 3.

Topics

Many topics provide children with opportunities for finding out about feeding. Some examples are:

OURSELVES	The sense of taste Cooking food to eat
SHOPS OR THE SUPERMARKET	Shopping for food Different types of food
FOOD	Similarities and differences between types of food Cooking Changes during cooking

The flow-diagram in section 1 (figure 3, pp.4–5) will help you identify further topics.

Classroom materials

The following Nelson Science materials support this unit:

Picture Resource Book 2

- p.4 – typical family meal: Korean family
- p.5 – typical family meal: British-origin white family
- p.6 – taking care of teeth

Science Discussion Books for key stage 1

- finding out about themselves and others and how to keep healthy

Science Explorers

- **Science Explorer, Carrying Out Surveys 1**
- **Science Explorer, Experimenting 1**
- **Science Explorer, Problem Solving 1**

Other useful materials from Nelson are:

- **Health for Life 1**
- **Health for Life 2**

Planning and Preparation

Related units
Children may ask questions which will provide opportunities for finding out about the content of other units. For example:

- growing and moving – unit 5
- using the senses – unit 6
- how to take care of plants – unit 8
- how to take care of animals – unit 11
- everyday substances which melt and solidify: ice/water, wax, chocolate etc. – unit 19

Resources and equipment
- samples of food to observe and taste, such as different vegetables and fruits etc; for example root vegetables, pulses, citrus fruits, exotic fruits, cereals and grains
- a hand lens or microscope for close observation work
- thermometer
- containers such as yogurt pots and coverings such as cling film
- ingredients for cooking

In the Classroom

Getting started

Starting points
Work on feeding can arise from:

children talking about:
- food they like or dislike
- food that they eat at home
- school meals
- the content of their lunch box

children using their senses to
- look closely at different types of food
- taste food

children visiting:
- a supermarket or shop
- a farm

children solving problems to:
- keep food fresh
- keep food cool

children reading/listening to stories such as:
- 'The Enormous Turnip'
- 'The Magic Porridge Pot'

Asking questions
The activities outlined above could lead to questions such as:

I wonder whether...
- people have favourite food?
- people from different cultures eat different food?
- families have the same meal times?
- food can be identified by taste alone?
- animals eat the same type of food as human beings?
- every part of a fruit or vegetable can be eaten?

What happens if...
- different food is exposed to air?
- different food is put in water?
- food is kept at different temperatures?

Can we find a way to...
- prevent food from rotting?

Gathering information
Encourage children to think of ways of **gathering information** to help answer these questions.

Investigations which might follow these questions are outlined on pp. 73–76.

Ideas for taking these investigations further are given below.

Further investigations

Carrying out surveys
Collecting information about:
- mealtimes and snack meals
– observe the ways in which we eat different foods; for example biting, sucking, chewing, licking
– record the amount of food we eat during one day, the times we eat and the meals we eat
– sort and group the wrappers and containers of food that we eat during one day or one week

Experimenting
- cooking and preserving different foods
- controlling the amount of sugar or fat when cooking.
– compare the results

Solving practical problems
- preparing a meal for a diabetic person
- preparing a meal for a baby

Handling information

Recording findings
Encourage the children to think about ways in which their findings can be recorded.

In the Classroom

Talk with the children about your reasons for choosing a particular method of recording.

Findings from practical problem-solving activities can be recorded through drawing and writing.

Findings from surveys and experiments can be recorded individually or as a group by:
- using simple charts and pictograms
- using tables and bar charts

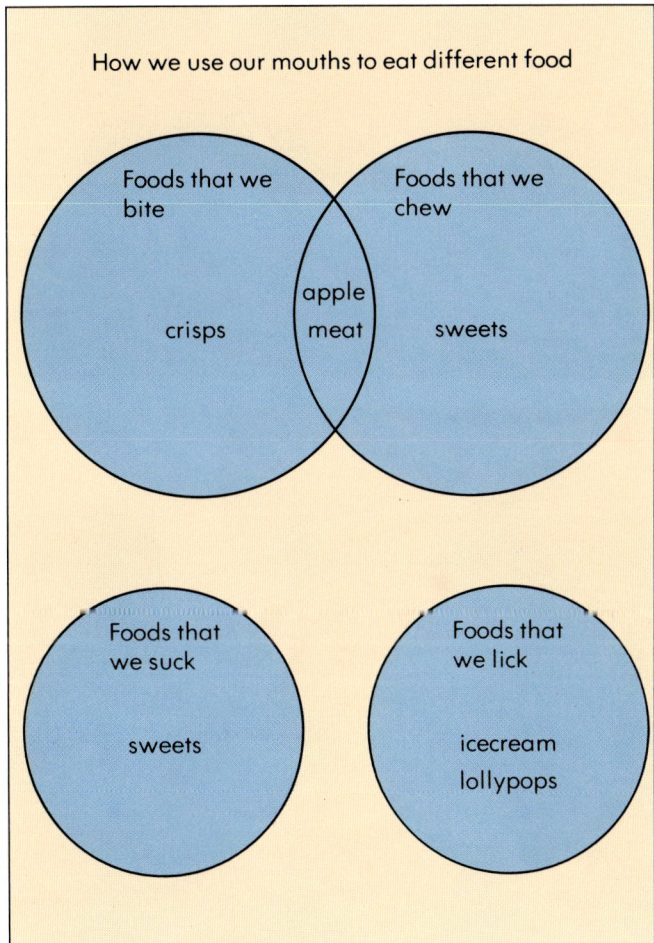

Interpreting findings
Encourage children to link findings and observations, and thus try to establish and express cause-and-effect relationships.

Record favourite foods onto a graph and interpret from the graph which is the overall favourite food or meal.

Review points
The following are useful talking points:

Our investigations
- the questions we asked
- how we planned
- how we collected information
- how and why we recorded
- what we found out

Making connections
- how eating certain foods is related to **dental care**
- food eaten by **different age groups and people**; for example, babies, who need milk and specially prepared food; diabetics, who need a carefully controlled diet
- **food chains** – how many foodstuffs go through different processes before we eat them.
- ways in which food is **preserved** both commercially and in the home; for instance, cooking, freezing, pickling, jam-making
- food as the **source of human energy**
- **people in countries where there is not enough food or water**, and the problems they face

Safety
Ensure that the children:
- carefully wash their hands before touching things to be put into their mouths
- are constantly supervised when they are tasting things
- are shown the correct way to use knives if they are cutting up food samples

Investigations

I wonder whether...
- **people have favourite foods?**
- **people from different cultures eat different foods?**

Children can **look at** a range of different food and meals. They should whenever possible have the opportunity to taste different food.

In the Classroom

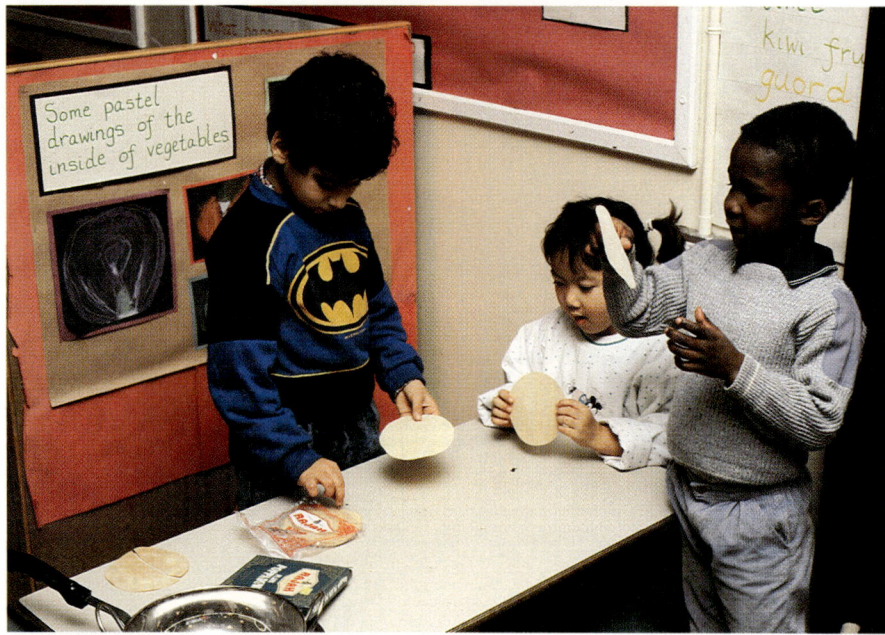

They could also **collect information** about preferences for food and also about similarities and differences in taste between children.

- **families have the same meal times?**

Children can **conduct surveys** to find out if they all have a meal before they come to school, and at what time they eat this meal.

They could also find out at what time they eat a meal after school.

- **food can be identified by taste alone?**

Children can try to **identify** the tastes of a variety of food when they are blindfolded and cannot smell or touch the food.

In the Classroom

- **animals eat the same type of food as human beings?**

Children can **conduct surveys** to find out what food pets eat.

They could also try to encourage different birds to visit the bird table by putting out different food.

- **every part of a fruit or vegetable can be eaten?**

Children can conduct surveys to find out which roots, seeds and leaves we eat.

What happens if . . .
- **different food is exposed to air?**

In the Classroom

Children can **observe** what happens to a vegetable such as a potato or an apple when it is exposed to air.

They could **discuss** how food is packaged and preserved for freshness and hygiene.

They could also **make a collection** of the different products made from potatoes and apples.

- **different food is put in water?**

Children can *find out* which things dissolve in water.

They could **talk about** drinks or foods that they eat which have things dissolved or mixed in them.

They could also **observe** any changes that happen when foods such as raw potato and apple are put into water.

They could **discuss** how different foods such as vegetables are prepared and kept fresh at home.

- **food is kept at different temperatures?**

Children can **collect information** about foods which are kept in refrigerators, freezers or cupboards.

They could put samples of food in cold places and warm places and **make observations** about the effect of temperature

Can we find a way to . . .

- **prevent food from rotting?**

The children could also **carry out surveys** about how food is packaged and preserved.

They could **discuss** how this keeps food fresh and helps us to keep healthy.

The children could also try to prevent vegetables, fruit and bread from deteriorating. They could:

– cook vegetables.
– make jam.
– cover food with different materials, such as wax paper, cling film and cooking foil.

Evaluation Checklist

Unit . . . .   Date . . . .

Teaching
Have the children been provided with opportunities to:

- work on questions or problems which they have accepted as their own? ☐
- work on questions or problems which have enabled them to:

AT3 – explore and talk about how they feed? ☐

AT3 – use books, pictures and charts to help in their explorations about how they keep healthy? ☐

AT4 – talk about similarities and differences between themselves and other children? ☐

AT13 – explore and talk about the foods they eat and why and when they eat them? ☐

Has the work pupils were engaged in allowed them to:

AT1 • talk about the purposes of recording results? ☐

AT1 • record results by drawing pictures, drawing block graphs and completing frequency charts, tables and bar charts? ☐

AT1 • sort and group objects and events such as: foods for a number of different criteria? ☐
  – children who like to eat vegetables and those who do not? ☐

AT1 • distinguish between a fair and an unfair test? ☐

AT1 • describe activities carried out by sequencing the major features? ☐

AT1 • discuss their observations and ideas with other children? ☐

AT1 • describe the best way of recording of their activities? ☐

AT1 • relate their findings to previous ideas and experiences? ☐

AT1 • reflect upon how their procedures might be improved? ☐

Learning
Have the children demonstrated that they can:

Level 1
AT3 • tell you the names of external parts of their body, such as arm, leg, head, nose, mouth? ☐

AT4 • talk to you about the ways in which they vary from one individual to the next; for example, in likes and dislikes in food? ☐

AT13 • tell you that they need food to be active? ☐

AT13 • talk to you about and draw pictures to show some of their daily activities and meal times? ☐

AT1 • make observations using their senses about food and feeding, and talk about their observations? ☐

Level 2
AT3 • tell you about hygiene and food being important in their daily lives? ☐

AT3 • talk to you about the routine of their own day? ☐

AT1 • identify simple variables such as hot/cold, raw/cooked? ☐

AT1 • ask questions and suggest ideas of the 'how' and 'why' variety? ☐

AT1 • record findings in charts and drawings? ☐

AT1 • list and collate observations? ☐

Level 3
AT3 • tell you the ways in which human beings and other living things feed? ☐

AT3 • talk to you about the main stages in the human life cycle? ☐

AT1 • formulate hypotheses? ☐

AT1 • distinguish between a fair and an unfair test? ☐

AT1 • record findings in tables and bar charts? ☐

AT1 • describe activities carried out by sequencing the major features? ☐

© Bishop Grosseteste College 1990. Copying permitted for purchasing school only. This material is not 'copyright free'

PLANTS

UNIT 8
HOW TO TAKE CARE OF PLANTS

Opportunities for learning

The range of suggestions in this unit provides children with the following opportunities from the **programme of study** for key stage 1:

- to explore a variety of plant life by taking responsibility for its care and welfare
- to develop their investigative skills and understanding of science in the context of explorations and investigations

The suggestions for practical activities and discussion outlined in this unit provide children with the experiences necessary to facilitate attainment up to level 3.

Topics

Many topics provide children with opportunities for finding out about how to take care of plants. Some examples are:

GROWTH	Rate of growth Variety of plants
THE HEDGEROW	Variety of plants – plants in danger of extinction – habitat
SPRING	Variety of plants – colour – shape – size – conditions
HARVEST	Variety of plants Growing seeds
FAIRYTALES such as 'Jack and the Beanstalk'	Rate of growth Variety of plants

The flow-diagram in section 1 (figure 3, pp.4–5) will help you identify further topics.

Classroom materials

The following Nelson Science materials support this unit:

Picture Resource Book 1

- p.4 – cacti
- p.5 – high-altitude plants
- p.6 – stages in a plant's growth
- p.7 – external parts of a plant
- p.10 – trees

Science Discussion Books for key stage 1

- finding out about plants

Planning and Preparation

Science Explorers
- **Science Explorer, Carrying Out Surveys 1**
- **Science Explorer, Experimenting 1**
- **Science Explorer, Problem Solving 1**

Related units

Children may ask questions which will provide opportunities for finding out about the content of other units. For example:

- light, shadows, colours and mirrors – unit 1
- improving the appearance of the local environment – unit 4
- how plant life varies – unit 9
- seasonal and daily changes in plants – unit 10

Resources and equipment

- a variety of common seeds, such as runner bean, sunflower, cress, tomato, horse chestnut and grass
- a range of growing media, such as soil, sand, peat and potting compost
- a selection of containers, such as yogurt pots, plant pots, polystyrene trays and saucers
- small-scale gardening tools, such as a trowel and dibber (or alternatively old cutlery is useful)
- measuring instruments, such as a thermometer
- a hand lens

In the Classroom

Getting started

Starting points
Work on how to take care of plants can arise from:

children reading/listening to stories such as:
- 'Jack and the Beanstalk'
- 'Little Red Hen'
- 'The Enormous Turnip'
- 'Joseph's Yard'

children visiting:
- a park
- a hedgerow
- a garden centre
- a farm or agricultural centre

children talking about:
- flowers growing in their gardens, or on the school field
- the names of the external parts of a plant
- plants, such as flowers, which smell good, and plants, such as wild garlic, which smell strong and unpleasant

children looking closely at:
- different seeds
- different plants
- flowers they have brought into the classroom

children making collections of:
- seeds
- plants
- gardening tools

Asking questions
The activities outlined above could lead to questions such as:

I wonder whether...
- seeds need water to grow?
- the amount of water given to a seed makes a difference?
- seeds need light to grow?
- seeds grow at the same rate?
- plants, such as flowers, live longer in the earth or in a vase of water?
- all plants need soil or compost to grow?
- the roots of a plant always grow down?

What happens if...
- seeds are grown in different media?
- seeds or bulbs are planted upside down?
- seeds or plants are kept in a warm place or a cold place?

Can we find a way to...
- collect seeds from a plant?
- grow plants in the classroom?
- transplant seedlings, grown in the classroom, into the garden?
- care for plants over a weekend or holiday?

Gathering information

Encourage children to think of ways of **gathering information** to help answer these questions.

Investigations which might follow these questions are outlined on pp.81–84.

Ideas for taking these investigations further are given below.

Further investigations

Carrying out surveys
Collecting information about:
- the variety of seeds
– explore the conditions needed to grow seeds successfully
– observe sort and group a variety of seeds
– observe the changes that happen when a seed, such as a bean, is grown
- the variety of plants
– investigate the conditions plants need to grow
– investigate plants that humans eat and plants that animals eat
– investigate how to handle plants

Experimenting
- growing plants from seed
– cover plants with different coloured paper
– compare the height of plants growing under different conditions
– control the conditions needed by plants, such as light, water, heat, and make observations about the results

Solving practical problems
- creating a suitable environment for plants
– set up and maintain a wild flower area
– construct a cold frame or mini-greenhouse
– care for plants over a weekend or holiday
– construct a device for controlling the amount of water given to a plant

In the Classroom

Handling information

Recording findings

Encourage the children to think about ways in which their findings can be recorded.

Talk with the children about your reasons for choosing a particular method of recording.

Findings from practical problem-solving activities can be recorded through drawing and writing.

Findings from surveys and experiments can be recorded individually or as a group by:

- using simple charts and pictograms
- using tables and bar charts

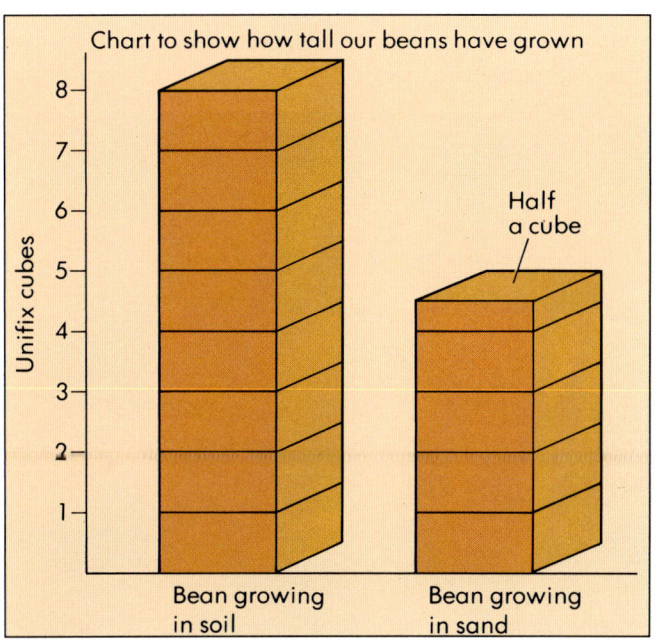

Interpreting findings

Encourage children to link findings and observations, and thus try to establish and express cause-and-effect relationships.

Help the children to link the amount of light with the rate of growth of a plant, and help them towards the knowledge that natural sunlight encourages plants to grow.

Review points

The following are useful talking points:

Our investigations

- the questions we asked
- how we planned
- how we collected information
- how and why we recorded
- what we found out

Making connections

- wild plants and flowers which are **in danger of extinction** and how we can care for them
- **exotic plants** which may need hot-house conditions to survive in this country
- plants that can grow from a **number of starting points**, such as seed, bulb, cutting and spore

Safety

Ensure that the children:

- know that some plants are poisonous
- wash their hands after handling plants

Investigations

I wonder whether . . .

- seeds need water to grow?
- **the amount of water given to a seed makes a difference?**

A fast-growing seed such as a bean or cress can be planted in a chosen growing medium in a number of

81

In the Classroom

containers. Children can vary the amount of water given to each one, ranging from no water at all to a lot of water.

They could begin to **collect information** about how much water a growing seed needs.

- **seeds need light to grow?**

Children can plant seeds in two containers. One container could be covered with black sugar paper and the other could be exposed to natural light.

Perhaps **discussion** with the children might lead to them deciding that it is fairer to give both containers the same amount of water, or they may decide that one container needs more water than the other.

- **seeds grow at the same rate?**

Children can **compare** the rate of growth of one type of seed grown under different conditions.

They could also **compare** the rate of growth of different seeds grown under one **controlled** condition.

Children may begin to **think about the variables** which might influence the results of this type of investigation.

- **plants, such as flowers, live longer in the earth or in a vase of water?**

Children often bring cut wild flowers or garden flowers into the classroom. **Comparisons** can be made between conditions necessary to keep cut flowers alive, and conditions that flowers have outside.

Children could **make observations** of changes that occur in cut flowers. Some flowers such as poppies wilt almost immediately, while others such as daisies or daffodils survive much longer.

Children could also talk about why plants have a root system.

- **all plants need soil or compost to grow?**

By **looking closely** at the places in which plants are found, children can **collect information** about how plants adapt to their environment.

In the Classroom

Plants such as marram grass, which can often be found at the coast, or weed, moss and lichen, which can be found on rocks and trees, can provide the stimulus for children to attempt to grow plants in soil, compost, sand or water.

- **the roots of a plant always grow down?**

Children can look at the root systems of a number of plants to find any similarities and differences.

By **observing** the root of a plant children can **gather information** about the purposes of the root system.

Perhaps children will also have experience of repotting plants or transplanting them to allow them to grow.

What happens if . . .
- **seeds are grown in different media?**

Children can **compare and measure** any differences in growth between seeds grown in soil, compost or a mixture of sand and soil.

- **seeds or bulbs are planted upside down?**

Children can **compare** seeds or bulbs which are planted upside down with those planted conventionally.

They could **observe** the effects and **collect information** about the rate of growth.

- **seeds or plants are kept in a warm place or a cold place?**

Children can **compare** the growth of seeds or plants which are kept under different conditions.

They could **make decisions** about where warm and cold places are.

Perhaps there will be an opportunity to talk about being fair; for instance, do both warm and cold places have the same amount of light?

83

In the Classroom

Can we find a way to...

- **collect seeds from a plant?**

Children can **collect** seeds from plants they find in hedgerows or gardens.

They can **discuss** which part of a plant to look for, and what times of the year would be best to try to find seeds.

They can **compare** the range of shapes and sizes of the seeds they find.

- **grow plants in the classroom?**

Children can **select** their own seeds for planting, or grow a plant taken from a cutting.

They could decide what they have to do so that they can take care of the living plant. A class or individuals could keep a **diary**, showing how the plant was looked after and how it grew.

This could provide another opportunity to **talk about** similarities and differences in plants, and about the variables involved in growing plants.

- **transplant seedlings, grown in the classroom, into the garden?**

By talking with the children about the needs of plants, decisions could be made about when to move plants grown from seed so they can have more space.

Children would then have to **find a way** to handle the seedlings without damaging them.

- **care for plants over a weekend or holiday?**

Children can place plant pots with drainage holes on a wet sponge, so that the plants receive water through the compost. Alternatively they could make a wick from cotton wool or rolled cotton fabric, soak it in water and place the other end in the compost, as shown.

Evaluation Checklist

Unit . . . .   Date . . . .

Teaching
Have the children been provided with opportunities to:

- work on questions or problems which they have accepted as their own? ☐

AT2
- work on questions or problems which have enabled them to:
  - observe and talk about a variety of plant life? ☐
  - take care of plants? ☐
  - explore and investigate the needs of plants? ☐

Has the work pupils were engaged in allowed them to:

AT1 • talk about the purposes of recording results? ☐

AT1 • record results by drawing pictures, drawing block graphs and completing frequency charts, tables and bar charts? ☐

AT1 • sort and group objects and events, such as:
  - seeds which are large and those which are not? ☐
  - seeds which grow into flowers and those which do not? ☐
  - plants which have flowers and those which do not? ☐

AT1 • measure using non-standard and simple-standard measuring skills; for instance:
  - the height of a growing plant? ☐
  - the amount of water given to a plant? ☐

AT1 • distinguish between a fair and an unfair test? ☐

AT1 • interpret findings by linking variables; for example, 'the plant growing in the light has grown 4 cm more than the plant growing in the dark'? ☐

AT1 • describe activities carried out by sequencing the major features? ☐

AT1 • discuss their observations and ideas with other children? ☐

AT1 • describe the best way of recording their activities? ☐

AT1 • relate their findings to previous ideas and experiences? ☐

AT1 • reflect upon how their procedures might be improved? ☐

Learning
Have the children demonstrated that they can:

Level 1
AT2 • recognise and talk about some of the similarities and differences between plants? ☐

AT1 • recognise and name the external parts of a plant, for example stem, leaf, flower? ☐

AT1 • make observations about the seeds or plants they are working with and talk abut them? ☐

Level 2
AT2 • describe the conditions, such as light, warmth and water, that plants need to survive? ☐

AT2 • look after plants and treat them with care and consideration? ☐

AT1 • identify simple variables such as tall/short, light/dark, wet/dry? ☐

AT1 • ask questions and suggest ideas of the 'how' and 'why' variety? ☐

AT1 • measure results using non-standard and standard units? ☐

AT1 • record findings in charts and drawings? ☐

AT1 • list and collate observations? ☐

AT1 • interpret findings by associating one factor with another, such as natural sunlight encouraging a plant to grow, or a plant dieing without water? ☐

Level 3
AT1 • formulate hypotheses? ☐

AT1 • distinguish between a fair and an unfair test? ☐

AT1 • measure using simple measuring instruments, such as a ruler, to the nearest labelled division? ☐

AT1 • record findings in tables and bar charts? ☐

AT1 • describe activities carried out by sequencing the major features? ☐

© Bishop Grosseteste College 1990. Copying permitted for purchasing school only. This material is not 'copyright free'.

PLANTS

UNIT 9
HOW PLANT LIFE VARIES

Opportunities for learning

The range of suggestions in this unit provides children with the following opportunities from the **programme of study** for key stage 1:

- to observe and explore a variety of plant life
- to develop their investigative skills and understanding of science in the context of explorations and investigations

The suggestions for practical activities and discussion outlined in this unit provide children with the experiences necessary to facilitate attainment up to level 3.

Topics

Many topics provide children with opportunities for finding out about how plant life varies. Some examples are:

HARVEST	Conditions needed by plants to grow Plants or parts of plants that are edible
THE SEASONS	How plants reproduce Similarities and differences among plants
GROWTH	Where plants grow Conditions needed by plants to grow

The flow-diagram in section 1 (figure 3, pp.4–5) will help you identify further topics.

Classroom materials

The following Nelson Science materials support this unit:

Picture Resource Book 1

- p.1 – seed head
- p.2 – pollen dispersal
- p.3 – animals that look like plants
- p.4 – cacti
- p.5 – high-altitude plants
- p.21 – desert conditions
- p.22 – tropical conditions

Science Discussion Books for key stage 1

- finding out about plants

Science Explorers

- **Science Explorer, Carrying Out Surveys 1**
- **Science Explorer, Problem Solving 1**

Planning and Preparation

Related units

Children may ask questions which will provide opportunities for finding out about the content of other units. For example:

- feeding – unit 7
- how to take care of plants – unit 8
- seasonal and daily changes in plants – unit 10

Resources and equipment

- a selection of common seeds, such as mustard and cress, grass, sunflowers and acorns
- a hand lens or magnifying glass
- a collection of leaves from different trees

In the Classroom

Getting started

Starting points
Work on how plant life varies can arise from:

children talking about:
- seeds and plants they have brought in
- plants they have seen in a particular place
- names of the different parts of a plant

children looking closely at:
- different seeds; for instance, sunflower seeds, conkers, apple pips and peach stones
- a variety of plants such as trees, wild flowers, garden flowers, grass, fungi and vegetables

children making collections of:
- a variety of seeds
- different coloured flowers
- different leaves found in autumn

children watching a television programme about:
- the range and variety of plant life

children reading/listening to stories such as:
- 'Meg's Veg'
- 'Jack and the Beanstalk'

Asking questions
The activities outlined above could lead to questions such as:

I wonder whether...
- all plants have leaves?
- all plants have roots?
- all plants have flowers?
- all plants have seeds?
- some plants grow on other plants?
- flowers have different parts to them?

Can we find a way to...
- collect and/or identify a variety of plants which grow in a small area?

Gathering information
Encourage children to think of ways of gathering information to help answer these questions.

Investigations which might follow these questions are outlined on pp.89–90.

Ideas for taking these investigations further are given below.

Further investigations

Carrying out surveys
Collecting information about:
- the variety of plant life
– Investigate the different plants that can be found in different environments; for instance, woodland, marsh, coast, river-bank, garden, waste ground
– observe and compare the growing conditions needed by plants
– compare the conditions that make plants grow well
– compare the growth of plants grown under different conditions, such as wet/dry or dark/light
– observe the similarities and differences between plants
– observe which part of a plant grows first
– compare trees which are evergreen or deciduous
– compare plants which flower and plants which bear fruit
– compare plants which are edible to humans and those which are edible to other animals
- the different parts of a plant
– count the number of petals on a flower, and compare this with other flowers
– count the number of points on a horse chestnut leaf, and compare this with other leaves
– compare the seeds that plants produce and how they are distributed

Solving practical problems
- collecting or identifying plants
– construct a quadrat frame

Handling information

Recording findings
Encourage the children to think about ways in which their findings can be recorded.

Talk with the children about your reasons for choosing a particular method of recording.

Findings from practical problem-solving activities can be recorded through drawing and writing.

Findings from surveys and experiments can be recorded individually or as a group by:
- using simple charts and pictograms
- using tables and bar charts

In the Classroom

Help the children to link the planting of a seed with the growth of the parent plant, and so come to the knowledge that living things reproduce their own kind.

Review points
The following are useful talking points:

Our investigations
- the questions we asked
- how we planned
- how we collected information
- how and why we recorded
- what we found out

Making connections
- the **growing conditions** needed by plants to sustain life
- the **similarities and differences between species** of plants; for example, between trees and flowers, grass and weeds
- the names of the **external parts of plants**
- the generic term 'plant', which covers organisms which draw nourishment from the air and soil
- plants which are found in **different environments;** for instance, seaweed, palm trees, cacti
- people with **occupations which are part of the food chain;** for example, farmers and market gardeners

Safety
Ensure that the children:
- know that some plants are poisonous
- wash their hands after handling plants

Investigations

I wonder whether...
- **all plants have leaves?**

Interpret findings
Encourage children to link findings and observations, and thus try to establish cause-and-effect relationships.

In the Classroom

- **all plants have roots?**

- **all plants have flowers?**

- **all plants have seeds?**

Children can **look at** as many different types of plant as possible throughout the year and in different environments.

Children can begin to collect detailed information about the wide variety of plant life.

- **some plants grow on other plants?**

Children can begin to **collect information** about the needs of growing plants.

They can **discriminate** between plants which grow in soil, plants such as fungi and lichen which grow on other plants, and plants such as mistletoe which is an evergreen parasitic plant.

- **flowers have different parts to them?**

By closely **observing** the flowers which are produced by different plants, children can begin to **collect information** about the wide variety of flowering plants. For instance, does the plant have a single flower head, or many flower heads attached to the stalk? What do the petals enclose? Are there leaves on the flowering plant?

Can we find a way to . . .

- **collect and/or identify a variety of plants which grow in a small area?**

Children can **construct** a simple quadrat frame from dowelling and cardboard triangles.

Alternatively, they could use a PE hoop, or a set ring.

Evaluation Checklist

Unit . . . .   Date . . . .

Teaching
Have the children been provided with opportunities to:

- • work on questions or problems which they have accepted as their own? ☐
- AT2 • work on questions or problems which have enabled them to:
  - – observe and talk about a variety of plant life? ☐

Has the work pupils were engaged in allowed them to:

- AT1 • talk about the purposes of recording results? ☐
- AT1 • record results by drawing pictures, drawing block graphs and completing frequency charts, tables and bar charts? ☐
- AT1 • sort and group objects and events, such as:
  - – trees that lose their leaves in autumn and those that do not? ☐
  - – plants that are edible and those that are not? ☐
- AT1 • measure using non-standard and simple standard measuring skills; for instance:
  - – the circumference of a tree trunk? ☐
  - – the relative height of plants? ☐
- AT1 • distinguish between a fair and an unfair test? ☐

Learning
Have the children demonstrated that they can:

Level 1
- AT2 • give examples of a wide variety of plants? ☐
- AT3 • name or label the external parts of plants; for example, flower, stem, leaf, root? ☐
- AT1 • make observations and talk about them? ☐

Level 2
- AT2 • describe the conditions plants need to live? ☐
- AT3 • explain some of the ways that plants reproduce; for example, seed dispersal? ☐
- AT1 • identify simple variables, such as tall/short, rough/smooth? ☐
- AT1 • ask questions and suggest ideas of the 'how' and 'why' variety? ☐
- AT1 • measure using non-standard and standard units? ☐
- AT1 • record findings in charts and drawings? ☐
- AT1 • list and collate observations? ☐

Level 3
- AT2 • recognise similarities and differences among plants? ☐
- AT2 • sort plants into groups according to observable features; for example, plants with smooth stalks, plants with flowers? ☐
- AT1 • formulate hypotheses? ☐
- AT1 • describe simple variables that change over time, such as the growth of a plant? ☐
- AT1 • distinguish between a fair and unfair test? ☐
- AT1 • measure using simple measuring instruments, such as a ruler, to the nearest labelled division? ☐
- AT1 • record findings in tables and bar charts? ☐
- AT1 • describe activities carried out by sequencing the major features? ☐

© Bishop Grosseteste College 1990. Copying permitted for purchasing school only. This material is not 'copyright free'.

PLANTS

UNIT 10
SEASONAL AND DAILY CHANGES IN PLANTS

Opportunities for learning

The range of suggestions in this unit provides children with the following opportunities from the **programme of study** for key stage 1:

- to explore a variety of plants and the effects on plants related to seasonal and daily changes
- to develop their investigative skills and understanding of science in the context of explorations and investigations

The suggestions for practical activities and discussion outlined in this unit provide children with the experiences necessary to facilitate attainment up to level 3.

Topics

Many topics provide children with opportunities for finding out about seasonal and daily changes in plants. Some examples are:

THE SEASONS	What happens to a tree in spring, summer, autumn, winter
TREES	Changes that happen over a year
SEEDS AND SEEDLINGS	Collecting, sorting and grouping a variety of seeds Planting and growing seeds

The flow-diagram in section 1 (figure 3, pp. 4–5) will help you identify further topics.

Classroom materials

The following Nelson Science materials support this unit:

Picture Resource Book 1

- p.9 – flower responding to daylight
- p.10 – trees in different seasons
- p.11 – life cycle of a flowering plant

Science Discussion Books for key stage 1

- finding out about plants

Science Explorers
- **Science Explorer, Carrying Out Surveys 1**

Related units

Children may ask questions which will provide opportunities for finding out about the content of other units. For example:

- How to take care of plants – unit 8
- How plant life varies – unit 9
- Changes in the weather and the effect of the weather – unit 14

Planning and Preparation

Resources and equipment

- a hand lens for close observational work
- measuring equipment such as rulers, tape-measures and a range of non-standard units (for example, Unifix cubes)
- a variety of seeds and seed heads, such as conkers, acorns and sunflowers

In the Classroom

Getting started

Starting points

Work on seasonal and daily changes in plants can arise from:

children talking about:
- seeds or leaves they have collected
- 'telling the time' from dandelion seed heads
- changes they have noticed in plants such as trees

children making collections of:
- conkers
- acorns
- other seeds
- leaves

children visiting:
- a park
- a hedgerow

children reading/listening to stories such as:
- 'The Selfish Giant'

Asking questions

The activities outlined above could lead to questions such as:

> **I wonder whether . . .**
> - all trees lose their leaves in autumn?
> - grass grows at the same rate all through the year?
> - some plants grow in certain seasons?
> - flowers open up their petals more when the sun is shining?

Gathering information

Encourage children to think of ways of gathering information to help answer these questions.

Investigations which might follow these questions are outlined on p.96.

Ideas for taking these investigations further are given below.

Further investigations

> **Carrying out surveys**
>
> **Collecting information about:**
>
> - seasonal changes in plants
> – observe plants such as trees which lose their leaves – when do the leaves start to fall, and what other changes happen to the leaves?
> – observe plants which produce seeds – when do they do this?
> – make comparisons between dandelions and other plants
> – observe plants which live for one growing season only
> – investigate how plants reproduce
> - daily changes in plants
> – observe and record growth rates and patterns
> – observe the length of time flowers survive on a plant
> – observe the length of time flower petals remain open

Handling information

Recording findings

Encourage the children to think about ways in which their findings can be recorded.

Talk with the children about your reasons for choosing a particular method of recording.

Findings from practical problem-solving activities can be recorded through drawing and writing.

Findings from surveys and experiments can be recorded individually or as a group by:

- using simple charts and pictograms
- using tables and bar charts

94

In the Classroom

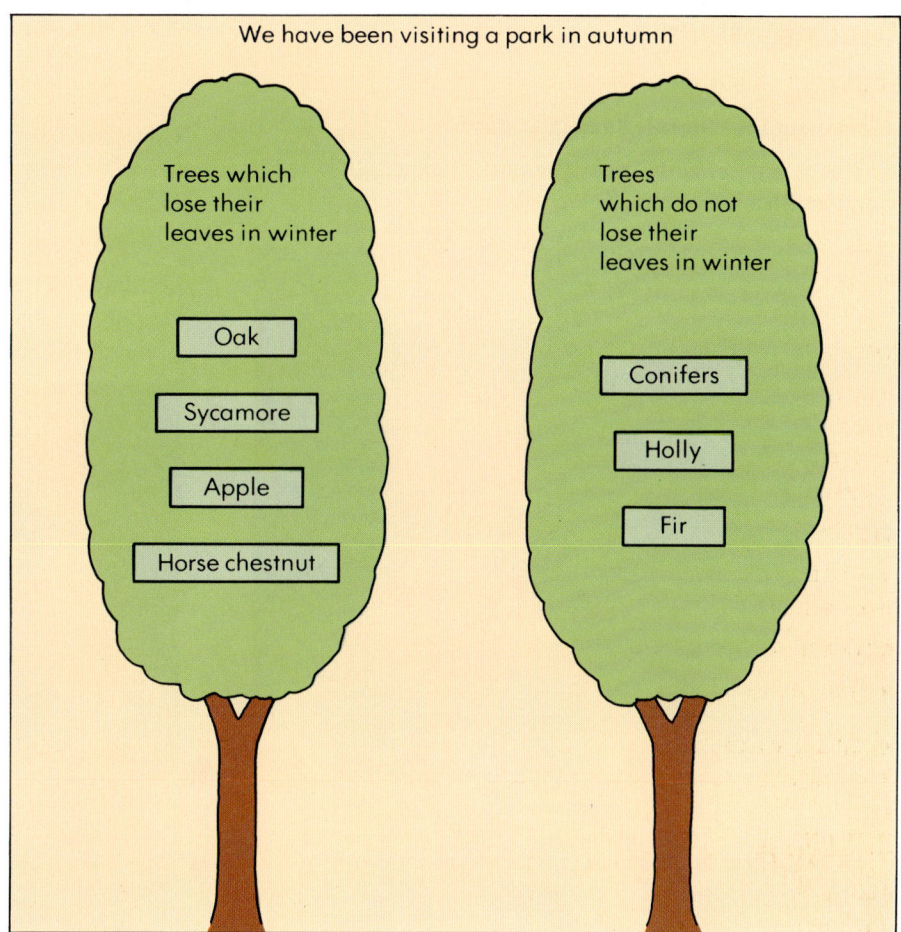

Interpreting findings
Encourage children to link findings and observations, and thus try to establish and express cause-and-effect relationships – for example, between the time of year (season) and the observed changes in a plant.

Review points
The following are useful talking points:

Our investigations
- the questions we asked
- how we planned
- how we collected information
- how and why we recorded
- what we found out

Making connections
- how daily and seasonal changes in the weather affect human beings and other animals

Safety
Ensure that the children:
- wash their hands after handling plants
- know that some plants are poisonous

In the Classroom

Investigations

I wonder whether...

- **all trees lose their leaves in autumn?**

Children can **closely observe** the changes that take place in the leaves on trees.

They could collect information about trees which lose their leaves in autumn and trees which do not lose their leaves in autumn.

- **grass grows at the same rate all through the year?**

Perhaps the children already have **experience** of helping their parents to cut the lawn at home. They can **collect information** about how often this is done.

A small area of grass in the school grounds could be left uncut over a period of time during the spring and summer.

Comparisons could be made between the rates of growth of the grass during the spring/summer and autumn/winter.

- **some plants grow in certain seasons?**

children can **collect information** from their garden, the school grounds, or the immediate local environment about the new plants which are growing.

They could begin to **link** the growth of certain plants with their growing season; for example, daffodils in spring, roses in summer.

- **flowers open up their petals more when the sun is shining?**

Children may **notice** that daisies which they find sometimes have closed petals.

Children can be encouraged to **find out** whether daisies growing in shaded places have closed or open petals, and whether this changes with the passage of the sun.

Perhaps children will **make connections** between this response of a daisy and the response of other plants they are observing; for example, plants with flowers that grow towards the sun.

Evaluation Checklist

Unit .... Date ....

Teaching
Have the children been provided with opportunities to:

- work on questions or problems which they have accepted as their own? ☐

AT16
- work on questions or problems which have enabled them to:
  - explore and talk about a variety of plants? ☐
  - explore and investigate some of the seasonal and daily changes that occur in plants? ☐

Has the work pupils were engaged in allowed them to:

AT1 • talk about the purposes of recording results? ☐

AT1 • record results by drawing pictures, drawing block graphs and bar charts? ☐

AT1 • sort and group objects and events, such as:
  - leaves, for a number of different criteria? ☐
  - trees which lose their leaves in autumn and trees which do not? ☐

AT1 • measure results using non-standard and simple standard measuring skills; for instance, how tall the uncut grass has grown in three weeks? ☐

AT1 • discuss their observations and ideas with other children? ☐

AT1 • describe the best way of recording their activities? ☐

AT1 • relate their findings to previous ideas and experiences? ☐

AT1 • reflect upon how their procedures might be improved? ☐

Learning
Have the children demonstrated that they can:

Level 1
AT16 • talk about the daily and seasonal changes that occur in plants? ☐

AT1 • make observations about seasonal and daily changes in plants and talk about them? ☐

Level 2
AT1 • identify simple variables such as tall/short, open/closed? ☐

AT1 • ask questions and suggest ideas of the 'how' and 'why' variety? ☐

AT1 • measure using non-standard and standard units? ☐

AT1 • record findings in charts and drawings? ☐

AT1 • list and collate observations? ☐

Level 3
AT1 • formulate hypotheses? ☐

AT1 • measure using simple measuring instruments, such as a ruler, to the nearest labelled division? ☐

AT1 • record findings in tables and bar charts? ☐

AT1 • interpret simple pictograms and bar charts? ☐

AT1 • describe activities carried out by sequencing the major features? ☐

© Bishop Grosseteste College 1990. Copying permitted for purchasing school only. This material is not 'copyright free'.

ANIMALS

UNIT 11
HOW TO TAKE CARE OF ANIMALS

Opportunities for learning

The range of suggestions in this unit provides children with the following opportunities from the **programme of study** for key stage 1:

- to care for animals by maintaining their welfare and knowing about their needs
- to develop their investigative skills and understanding of science in the context of explorations and investigations

The suggestions for practical activities and discussion outlined in this unit provide children with the experiences necessary to facilitate attainment up to level 3.

Topics

Many topics provide children with opportunities for finding out about how to take care of animals. Some examples are:

PETS	Similarities and differences How to take care of different pets
THE CIRCUS	How animals are cared for
THE SEASONS	How to look after animals; for example, butterflies
THE ZOO	Needs of different animals

The flow-diagram in section 1 (figure 3, pp.4–5) will help you identify further topics.

Classroom materials

Picture Resource Book 2

- p.17 – care of endangered animals in zoos
- p.18 – animals in their natural habitats

Science Discussion Books for key stage 1

- finding out about animals

Science Explorers

- **Science Explorer, Carrying Out Surveys 1**
- **Science Explorer, Experimenting 1**
- **Science Explorer, Problem Solving 1**

Related units

Children may ask questions which will provide opportunities for finding out about the content of other units. For example:

- feeding – unit 7
- how animal life varies – unit 12
- seasonal and daily changes in animals – unit 13

Planning and Preparation

Resources and equipment
Equipment for collecting and handling animals, such as:
- nets
- sieves
- containers
- a hand lens
- trays or boxes
- polythene bags
- an aquarium
- suitable food for animals

In the Classroom

Getting started

Starting points
Work on how to take care of animals can arise from:

children talking about:
- their pets
– what their pets eat
– where their pets sleep
- animal tracks they have seen

children visiting:
- a zoo
- a farm
- a circus

children looking after animals in the classroom such as:
- the class rabbit or gerbil
- chicks in an incubator
- caterpillars and butterflies

children watching a television programme about:
- pets, zoos or taking care of wildlife

children reading/listening to stories such as:
- 'The Tiger Who Came to Tea'
- 'The Town Mouse and the Country Mouse'

Asking questions
The activities outlined above could lead to questions such as:

> **I wonder whether . . .**
> - **all animals eat the same food?**
> - **all animals have the same coat?**
> - **some animals have favourite places to live?**
> - **all animals need the same things?**

> **What happens if . . .**
> - **fertilised eggs are kept in an incubator?**

> **Can we find a way to . . .**
> - **find or make a suitable habitat for an animal?**

Gathering information
Encourage children to think of ways of **gathering information** to help answer these questions.

Investigations which might follow these questions are outlined on pp. 101–104.

Ideas for taking these investigations further are given below.

Further investigations

> **Carrying out surveys**
> **Collecting information about:**
> - **the needs of pets**
> – investigate the best way of looking after a pet
> – observe the similarities and differences between pet animals
> – investigate the number and range of different pets
> - **caring for wild animals**
> – caring for domesticated farm animals
> – compare the needs of different animals in zoos and on farms
> – look for creatures around the school grounds
> – sort and group animals for a number of different criteria; for example, number of legs, what they eat, where they live

> **Experimenting**
> - **creating different environments for minibeasts**
> – find out about the living conditions needed by woodlice

> **Solving practical problems**
> - **constructing a home for minibeasts**
> – ensure that the basic needs of warmth, food, shelter and ventilation are met

Handling information

Recording findings
Encourage the children to think about ways in which their findings can be recorded.

Talk with the children about your reasons for choosing a particular method of recording.

Findings from practical problem-solving activities can be recorded through drawing and writing.

In the Classroom

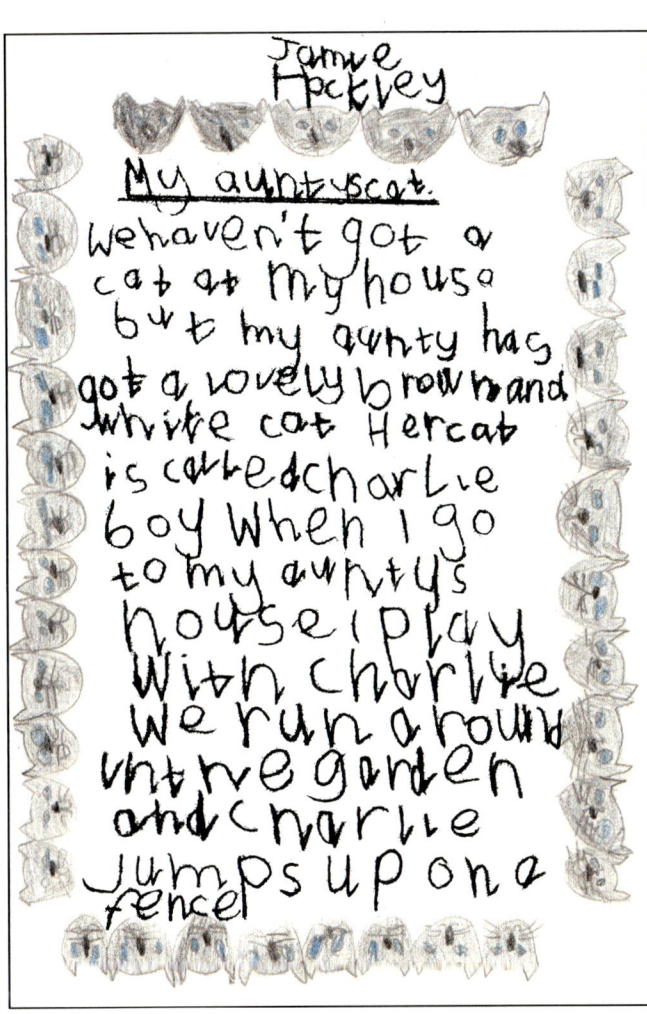

Findings from surveys and experiments can be recorded individually or as a group by:
- using simple charts and pictograms
- using tables and bar charts

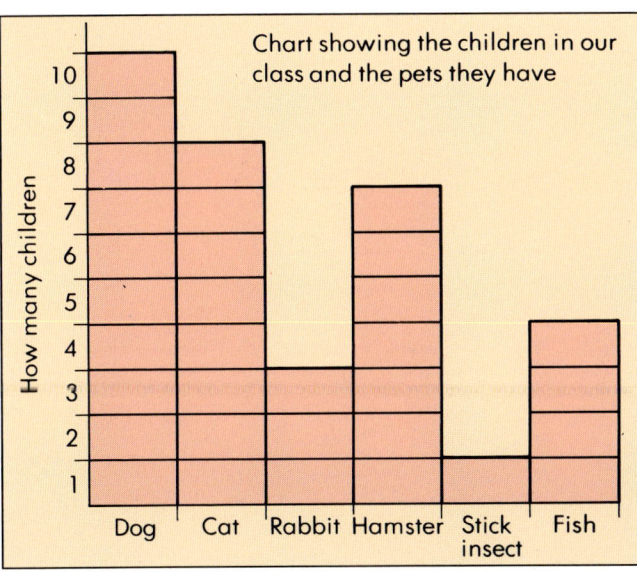

Interpreting findings

Encourage children to link findings and observations, and thus try to establish and express cause-and-effect relationships – for example, between the actions of human beings and the well-being of animals.

Review points

The following are useful talking points:

Our investigations
- the questions we asked
- how we planned
- how we collected information
- how and why we recorded
- what we found out

Making connections
- **similarities and differences in the needs of:**
- animals which are **wild**, ranging from birds to large mammals
- animals which have been **domesticated**, such as cattle
- animals which we keep as **pets**

Safety

Ensure that the children:
- wash their hands after handling animals
- are not allergic to certain animals that may be brought into the classroom; for example, birds and cats
- have any animal bites or scratches treated promptly and carefully
- do not handle animals if the children have open wounds or any infection

Investigations

I wonder whether . . .
- **all animals eat the same food?**

The children can **take surveys** about the type of food their pets eat.

In the Classroom

They could **collect information** about animals' food preferences. They could **observe** which birds visit the bird table when currants, bread, seed, or apple cores are put out; or find out whether rabbits prefer to eat fresh dandelion leaves or dried food.

- **all animals have the same coat?**

The children can **use their sense of touch** to find out whether cats, rabbits and dogs have coats which are the same. The could **compare** these to the feel of a sheep's fleece.

They could **carry out surveys** of how pet owners take care of their animals' coats.

They could also investigate how birds and fish differ from mammals in the type of coat' they have.

- **some animals have favourite places to live?**

In the Classroom

By observing different animals in their natural environment, children can begin to **collect information** about the habitats of animals such as minibeasts and birds.

Children could **discuss** why it is important to take care of the local natural environment so that the habitats of such animals are preserved.

- **all animals need the same things?**

Children can **collect information** about which pets and other animals need places where they can hibernate.

They could **investigate** how to take care of an animal like a tortoise which hibernates.

What happens if . . .
- **fertilised eggs are kept in an incubator?**

In the Classroom

The children can **take responsibility** for caring for the eggs, and then caring for and carefully handling the newly hatched chicks.

Can we find a way to . . .

- **find or make a suitable habitat for an animal?**

The children can use everyday materials to **construct** a suitable environment for minibeasts.

They could also make a wormery.

Evaluation Checklist

Unit .... Date ....

Teaching

Have the children been provided with opportunities to:

- work on questions or problems which they have accepted as their own? ☐
- AT2 • work on questions or problems which have enabled them to:
  - care for animals over a period of time? ☐
  - find out about the needs of animals? ☐

Has the work pupils were engaged in allowed them to:

- AT1 • talk about the purposes of recording results? ☐
- AT1 • record results by drawing pictures, drawing block graphs and completing frequency charts, tables and bar charts? ☐
- AT1 • sort and group objects and events, such as:
  - animals which eat meat and animals which do not? ☐
  - animals which make good pets and animals which do not? ☐
- AT1 • describe activities carried out by sequencing the major features? ☐
- AT1 • discuss their observations and ideas with other children? ☐
- AT1 • describe the best way of recording their activities? ☐
- AT1 • relate their findings to previous ideas and experiences? ☐
- AT1 • reflect upon how their procedures might be improved? ☐
- AT1 • act in a safe and careful way? ☐

Learning

Have the children demonstrated that they can:

Level 1
- AT1 • make observations about how to take care of animals and talk about them? ☐

Level 2
- AT2 • talk about the conditions animals need to survive? ☐
- AT2 • tell you about how animals are looked after? ☐
- AT2 • treat and handle animals with care and consideration? ☐
- AT1 • ask questions of the 'how' and 'why' variety? ☐
- AT1 • record findings in charts and drawings? ☐
- AT1 • list and collate observations? ☐

Level 3
- AT1 • formulate hypotheses? ☐
- AT1 • record findings in tables and bar charts? ☐
- AT1 • describe activities carried out by sequencing the major features? ☐

© Bishop Grosseteste College 1990. Copying permitted for purchasing school only. This material is not 'copyright free'.

ANIMALS

UNIT 12
HOW ANIMAL LIFE VARIES

Opportunities for learning

The range of suggestions in this unit provides children with the following opportunities from the **programme of study** for key stage 1:

- to explore and investigate the variety of animal life
- to develop their investigative skills and understanding of science in the context of explorations and investigations

The suggestions for practical activities and discussion outlined in this unit provide children with the experiences necessary to facilitate attainment up to level 3.

Topics

Many topics provide children with opportunities for finding out about how animal life varies. Some examples are:

PETS	Similarities and differences
ANIMALS IN THE ZOO	Variety of animal life
MINIBEASTS	Similarities and differences. Habitats of animals

The flow-diagram in section 1 (figure 3, pp.4–5) will help you identify further topics.

Classroom materials

The following Nelson Science materials support this unit:

Picture Resource Book 2

- p.8 – common insect
- p.9 – fish
- p.10 – bird with young
- p.11 – snake
- p.12 – cat with young

Science Discussion Books for key stage 1

- finding out about animals

Science Explorers
- **Science Explorer, Carrying Out Surveys 1**
- **Science Explorer, Problem Solving 1**

Related units

Children may ask questions which will provide opportunities for finding out about the content of other units. For example:

- how to take care of animals – unit 8
- seasonal and daily changes in animals – unit 10

Planning and Preparation

Resources and equipment
- a hand lens or magnifying glass for close observation
- collecting and specimen jars
- materials for designing and making homes for animals, such as a glass tank, a large jar, different coloured soils, sand, peat, chalk

In the Classroom

Getting started

Starting points
Work on how animal life varies can arise from:

children talking about:
- their pets

children visiting:
- a circus
- a zoo

children looking closely at and collecting animals from:
- a pond
- a stream

children watching a television programme about:
- pets, zoos or taking care of wildlife

children reading/listening to stories such as:
- 'Longneck and Thunderfoot'
- 'The Village Dinosaur'
- 'What-a-Mess'
- 'The Church Mice'

Asking Questions
The activities outlined above could lead to questions such as:

> **I wonder whether...**
> - some animals live in one place and not another?
> - all animals have the same number of legs?
> - all animals have the same number of eyes?
> - all animals move in the same way?
> - all animals eat the same type of food?
> - children in the class have pets of their own?

> **Can we find a way to...**
> - make a home for
>   – worms?
>   – snails?
>   – butterflies?
> - catch animals for investigation without harming them?

Gathering information
Encourage children to think of ways of **gathering information** to help answer these questions.

Investigations which might follow these questions are outlined on pp.109–112.

Ideas for taking these investigations further are given below.

Further investigations

> **Carrying out surveys**
> Collecting information about:
> - a pet
> – systematically collect and record measurements of one pet animal, such as a kitten or classroom pet.
> – record length, weight and amount of food it eats
> - birds
> – investigate the favourite food of birds

> **Solving practical problems**
> - constructing a bird scarer which will not harm the animals

Handling Information

Recording findings
Encourage the children to think about ways in which their findings can be recorded.

Talk with the children about your reasons for choosing a particular method of recording.

Findings from practical problem-solving activities can be recorded through drawing and writing.

In the Classroom

There were some very big moths on a plant. They were much bigger than my hands

Findings from surveys and experiments can be recorded individually or as a group by:

- using simple charts and pictograms
- using tables and bar charts

We have been talking about the animals we have seen	
Animals which can fly	Animals which cannot fly
Owl	Dog
Bat	Fish
Ladybird	Cat
Butterfly	Penguin
	Stick insect
	Human
	Mouse

Interpreting findings

Encourage children to link findings and observations, and thus try to establish and express cause-and-effect relationships – for example, between the way in which an animal moves and the shape of its whole body and/or parts of the body.

Review points

Our investigations

- the questions we asked
- how we planned
- how we collected information
- how and why we recorded
- what we found out

Making connections

- animals which are **wild** and animals which are **domesticated**
- animals which are indigenous to **other countries**
- animals which are in danger of becoming extinct or have become extinct.
- **environmental factors** involved in supporting animal life

Safety

Ensure that the children:

- always wash their hands after handling animals
- are not allergic to certain animals
- have any animal bite, sting or scratch immediately and carefully treated

Investigations

I wonder whether . . .

- **some animals live in one place and not another?**

Encourage the children to look carefully at animals found in different environments.

In the Classroom

They could sort and classify the animals found in: a stream or pond, the hedgerow, a farm, or a zoo.

They could also talk about their pets and the different homes their pets have. They can discuss why some animals would not make good pets.

- **all animals have the same number of legs?**
- **all animals have the same number of eyes?**

Children can carefully **observe** a variety of animals found in the local environment, and **sort and classify** the animals.

- **all animals move in the same way?**

Children can **discuss** how different animals move. They can **sort** them into animals which move in one way only (for example, fish) and animals which move in more than one way (for example, a duck).

In the Classroom

- **all animals eat the same type of food?**

The children could **sort** animals into groups which eat certain types of food; for example, meat-eaters, seed-eaters, grass-eaters.

- **children in the class have pets of their own?**

Talk with the children about their own pets. Children can closely observe their pets and talk about how they are similar/different, what the needs of their pets are and how they look after them.

In the Classroom

Can we find a way to...

- **make a home for worms?**

Children can **prepare a** glass tank or large jar filled with equal quantities of different coloured soils, sand and soil, peat and soil or chalk and soil. Put in several worms and cover the container with black paper.

Keep the soil moist and **observe** the worms regularly.

Fresh leaves, seeds and pieces of vegetables could be placed on the surface and **examined** every few days.

- **make a home for snails?**

The children can keep snails in the classroom in a box of damp soil or in a simple vivarium made from a perspex or glass tank.

The snails need to be given a variety of leaves including lettuce, dandelion and rhubarb.

- **make a home for butterflies?**

Children can use a large jar to **make** a home for butterflies. If the food plant is small it can be dug up and transplanted into a yogurt carton.

If the surface soil is covered with polythene or aluminium foil, evaporation is restricted and less watering is necessary.

Alternatively a small water-pot can be used as illustrated. The lid of the jar must be perforated to allow ventilation and the escape of excess water vapour.

Do not wait for the food to wilt before putting in fresh.

- **catch animals for investigation without harming them?**

Encourage the children to **think about** ways to make sure that they do not harm the animals they catch.

This will include ways of carefully transferring the animals from the environment and to and from collecting containers, and ways of keeping the animals alive and well in the classroom.

Evaluation Checklist

Unit . . . .   Date . . . .

Teaching
Have the children been provided with opportunities to:

- work on questions or problems which they have accepted as their own? ☐
- AT2 • work on questions or problems which have enabled them to:
  - observe and talk about a variety of different animals? ☐
  - use books, stories, pictures, charts and videos to find out about a variety of different animals? ☐

Has the work pupils were engaged in allowed them to:

- AT1 • talk about the purposes of recording results? ☐
- AT1 • record results by drawing pictures, drawing block graphs and completing frequency charts, tables and bar charts? ☐
- AT1 • sort and group objects, such as:
  - animals which swim and animals which do not swim? ☐
  - animals with four legs and animals that do not have four legs? ☐
- AT1 • describe activities carried out by sequencing the major features? ☐
- AT1 • discuss their observations and ideas with other children? ☐
- AT1 • describe the best way of recording their activities? ☐
- AT1 • relate their findings to previous ideas and experiences? ☐
- AT1 • reflect upon how their procedures might be improved? ☐

Learning
Have the children demonstrated that they can:

Level 1
- AT2 • talk to you about a variety of different animals? ☐
- AT2 • tell you that animals are living things? ☐
- AT1 • make observations of animals and talk about their observations? ☐

Level 2
- AT2 • tell you about the conditions different animals need to survive? ☐
- AT3 • tell you that animals reproduce their own kind? ☐
- AT1 • ask questions and suggest ideas of the 'how' and 'why' variety? ☐
- AT1 • record findings in charts and drawings? ☐
- AT1 • list and collate observations? ☐

Level 3
- AT2 • tell you about some of the similarities and differences between animals? ☐
- AT2 • observe, sort and group animals for a number of different criteria? ☐
- AT4 • talk about some of the animals which have now became extinct? ☐
- AT1 • formulate hypotheses? ☐
- AT1 • record findings in tables and bar charts? ☐
- AT1 • interpret findings in pictograms and bar charts? ☐
- AT1 • describe activities carried out by sequencing the major features? ☐
- AT1 • select and use simple measuring instruments, such as a hand lens, to enhance observations? ☐
- AT1 • identify and describe simple variables that change over time, such as the growth of an animal? ☐

© Bishop Grosseteste College 1990. Copying permitted for purchasing school only. This material is not 'copyright free'.

ANIMALS

UNIT 13
SEASONAL AND DAILY CHANGES IN ANIMALS

Opportunities for learning

The range of suggestions in this unit provides children with the following opportunities from the **programme of study** for key stage 1:

- to investigate the changes that occur in animals because of seasonal and daily changes
- to develop their investigative skills and understanding of science in the context of explorations and investigations

The suggestions for practical activities and discussion outlined in this unit provide children with the experiences necessary to facilitate attainment up to level 3.

Topics

Many topics provide children with opportunities for finding out about seasonal and daily changes in animals. Some examples are:

PETS	Changes in animals' coats Hibernation
THE SEASONS	Animals in the environment Bird migration
THE WEATHER	Animal hibernation Bird migration

The flow-diagram in section 1 (figure 3, pp.4–5) will help you identify further topics.

Classroom materials

The following Nelson Science materials support this unit:

Picture Resource Book 2

- p.10 – nocturnal animals
- p.13 – life cycle of a frog
- p.15 – hibernating animals
- p.16 – life cycle of a butterfly

Science Discussion Books for key stage 1

- finding out about animals

Science Explorers

- **Science Explorer, Carrying Out Surveys 1**
- **Science Explorer, Problem Solving 1**

Related units

Children may ask questions which will provide opportunities for finding out about the content of other units.

Planning and Preparation

For example:
- how to take care of animals – unit 11
- how animal life varies – unit 12

Resources and equipment
- a hand lens for close observation work
- nets
- specimen jars
- bird food

In the Classroom

Getting started

Starting points
Work on seasonal and daily changes in animals can arise from:

children talking about:
- their pets; for example:
– hamsters being active in the evening
– the coats of dogs and horses becoming thicker in winter
- feeding birds

children making observations of:
- birds visiting the birdtable
- seasonal animals such as butterflies and tadpoles

children visiting:
- a hedgerow
- a pond

Children reading/listening to stories such as:
- 'Goodnight Owl'
- 'The Owl who was Afraid of the Dark'

Asking questions
The activities outlined above could lead to questions such as:

I wonder whether . . .
- our pets like the rain?
- our pets stay indoors during the winter?
- animals' coats stay the same all year round?
- the same sort of birds visit the bird table all year round?
- some animals hibernate when the weather is cold?

Can we find a way to . . .
- take care of an animal which hibernates, such as a tortoise?

Gathering information
Encourage children to think of ways of **gathering information** to help answer these questions.

Investigations which might follow these questions are outlined on pp. 118–120.

Ideas for taking these investigations further are given below.

Further investigations

Carrying out surveys
Collecting information about:
- what happens to animals at night
– collect information about diurnal and nocturnal animals
– sort and group animals which are nocturnal and those which are not
- how some animals prepare for winter
– observe animals in the environment and collect information about their habitats and food source
– sort and group animals which migrate or hibernate and those which do not
- daily and seasonal changes that affect animals
- discuss changes between day and night
– discuss seasonal changes in the weather
– use their senses to describe the changes
– keep a diary and record the changes that happen to animals in the environment

Handling information

Recording findings
Encourage the children to think about ways in which their findings can be recorded.

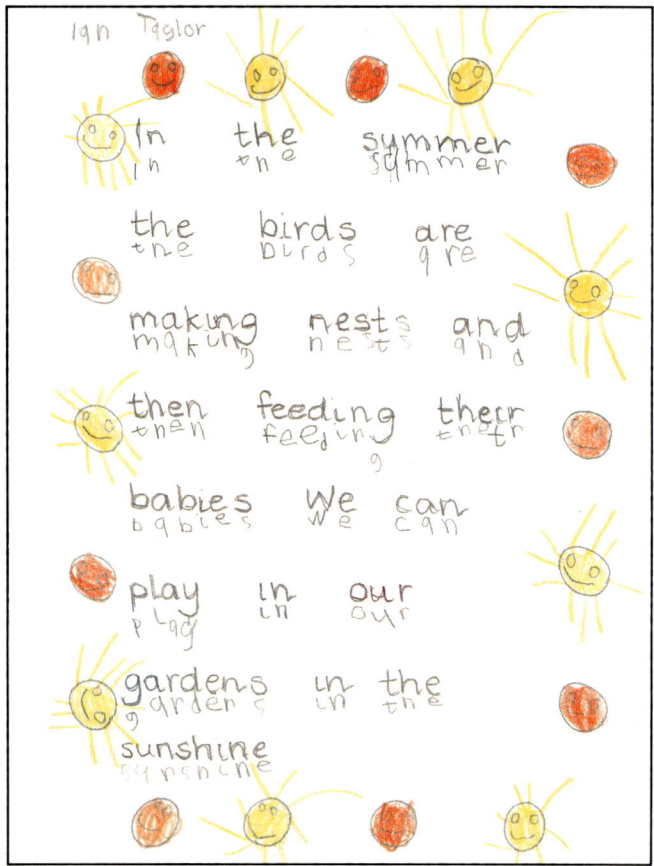

In the Classroom

Talk with the children about your reasons for choosing a particular method of recording.

Findings from practical problem-solving activities can be recorded through drawing and writing.

Findings from surveys and experiments can be recorded individually or as a group by:

- using simple charts and pictograms
- using tables and bar charts

Birds which visit our bird table	
Sparrow	XXXXXXXXXXXXXX
Blackbird	XXX
Gull	XXXXXXXXXX
Robin	X

Interpreting findings
Encourage children to link findings and observations, and thus try to establish and express cause-and-effect relationships – for example, those between the time of year (season) and the observed changes in animals' behaviour and appearance.

Review points
The following are useful talking points:

Our investigations
- the questions we asked
- how we planned
- how we collected information
- how and why we recorded
- what we found out

Making connections
- how a variety of animals respond to **seasonal changes**; for example, what happens to birds and butterflies in winter
- how animals respond to **daily changes**; for example, why some animals, such as owls and hedgehogs, sleep during the day
- animals which **hibernate**, and why

In the Classroom

Safety
Ensure that the children:
- wash their hands thoroughly after handling animals
- do not bring wild animals into the school
- carefully store any food for animals

Investigations

I wonder whether . . .
- **our pets like the rain?**

The children can talk and collect information about the habits of pets during different weather conditions.

In the Classroom

- **our pets stay indoors during the winter?**

The children can discuss how their pets are cared for during the winter.

They could find out whether pets such as cats or dogs go outdoors less in winter than summer.

- **animals' coats stay the same all year round?**

Some animals, such as horses and dogs, grow thicker coats during the winter months. The children can observe, by looking and touching, the condition of these animals' coats.

Some animals, such as sheep, have their coats cut or sheared in the spring. The children could talk about why they think this is necessary.

- **the same sort of birds visit the bird table all year round?**

The children can observe and keep a diary of the types of bird which visit the bird table during the year.

In the Classroom

They could **observe** other birds which are only seen in the local, natural environment during certain seasons; for example, swifts, bluetits.

- **some animals hibernate when the weather is cold?**

Some children may have previous experience of their pets hibernating.

They can share their experiences with the other children, **talking** about why their pets hibernate.

The children could look closely in their local natural environment for signs of animals hibernating.

Can we find a way to . . .

- take care of an animal which hibernates, such as a tortoise?

The children can **discuss** why animals hibernate.

They could **prepare a habitat** with suitable conditions so that the animal will survive hibernation.

Tortoises are plant eaters, and need to be given cabbage, lettuce and dandelion leaves, and pieces of carrot or parsnip. They must have clean water in a heavy shallow dish.

In the autumn they must be provided with a large box filled with hay and perforated for ventilation. The box is best placed in an unheated room such as a garage or outbuilding.

Tortoises must not be disturbed during hibernation.

Evaluation Checklist

Unit .... Date ....

Teaching
Have the children been provided with opportunities to:

- work on questions or problems which they have accepted as their own? ☐

AT16
- work on questions or problems which have enabled them to:
    - observe animals in their local, natural environment? ☐
    - explore how animals are affected by daily and seasonal changes? ☐

Has the work pupils were engaged in allowed them to:

AT1 • talk about the purposes of recording results? ☐

AT1 • record results by drawing pictures, drawing block graphs and completing frequency charts, tables and bar charts? ☐

AT1 • sort and group objects and events, such as:
    - animals which are nocturnal and those which are not? ☐

AT1 • discuss their observations and ideas with other children? ☐

AT1 • relate their findings to previous ideas and experiences? ☐

AT1 • reflect upon how their procedures might be improved? ☐

Learning
Have the children demonstrated that they can:

Level 1
AT16 • tell you about the seasonal changes that occur in the weather? ☐

AT16 • talk to you about how animals are affected by daily and seasonal changes? ☐

AT1 • make observations of animals to detect changes in them and talk about their observations? ☐

Level 2
AT1 • identify simple variables such as hot/cold? ☐

AT1 • ask questions and suggest ideas of the 'how' and 'why' variety? ☐

AT1 • record findings in charts and drawings? ☐

AT1 • list and collate observations? ☐

Level 3
AT1 • formulate hypotheses? ☐

AT1 • record findings in tables and bar charts? ☐

AT1 • describe activities carried out by sequencing the major features? ☐

Bishop Grosseteste College 1990. Copying permitted for purchasing school only. This material is not 'copyright free'.

SKY AND WEATHER

UNIT 14
CHANGES IN THE WEATHER AND THE EFFECT OF THE WEATHER

Opportunities for learning

The range of suggestions in this unit provides children with the following opportunities from the **programme of study** for key stage 1:

- to explore the ways in which the weather affects our lives
- to explore seasonal changes in the weather
- to develop their investigative skills and understanding of science in the context of explorations and investigations

The suggestions for practical activities and discussion outlined in this unit provide children with the experiences necessary to facilitate attainment up to level 3.

Topics

Many topics provide children with opportunities for finding out about changes in the weather and the effect of the weather. Some examples are:

THE WEATHER	Daily changes Seasonal variations Meteorological symbols
CLOTHES	Similarities and differences Fabrics to wear on hot/cold days Fabrics to wear on dry/wet days
WATER	Rainy day things
BUILDINGS	Effects of weathering

The flow-diagram in section 1 (figure 3, pp.4–5) will help you identify further topics

Classroom materials

The following Nelson science materials support this unit:

Picture Resource Book 1

- p.17 – effects of severe weather conditions
- p.18 – meteorological symbols
- p.19 – seasonal variations in weather

Science Discussion Books for key stage 1

- finding out about sky and weather

Planning and Preparation

Science Explorers

- Science Explorer, Carrying Out Surveys 1
- Science Explorer, Experimenting 1
- Science Explorer, Problem Solving 1

Related units

Children may ask questions which will provide opportunities for finding out about the content of other units. For example:

- changes in temperature: hot and cold – unit 16
- feeding – unit 7
- how to make things move – unit 17
- everyday substances which melt and solidify: ice/water, wax, chocolate etc. – unit 19

Resources and equipment

- a selection of open-and-close weave fabrics such as different wools and cottons
- a selection of natural and manufactured fabrics such as wool, cotton, PVC, nylon
- clear containers (bowls and jugs)
- construction materials to make a rain gauge or a wind sock – a tube of fabric, a wire hoop and a pole
- cookery ingredients for food such as soup, porridge, ice cream

In the Classroom

Getting started

Starting points

Work on changes in the weather and the effect of the weather can arise from:

children using their senses to observe:
- the sky
- the wind
- the rain
- the sun

children talking about:
- their clothes
- how they keep warm
- how they keep cool
- food they eat in different seasons

children solving problems to:
- stop objects sliding
- make objects slide

children reading/listening to stories such as:
- 'The Sun and the Wind'
- 'The Wind Blew'

Asking questions

The activities outlined above could lead to questions such as:

> **I wonder whether...**
> - the clouds look the same every day?
> - the wind blows from the same direction every day?
> - when it rains or snows, the same amount falls every day?
> - we always need to wear extra clothes when we are outside?
> - we eat different food at different times of the year?
> - some fabrics are warmer than others?

> **What happens if...**
> - different fabrics get wet?

> **Can we find a way to...**
> - stop things sliding on ice?

Gathering information

Encourage children to think of ways of gathering information to help answer these questions.

Investigations which might follow these questions are outlined on pp. 126–128.

Ideas for taking these investigations further are given below.

Further investigations

> **Carrying out surveys**
> Collecting information about:
> - making observations and describing the weather today
> – observe what clouds are like, whether they move, and if so in which direction they move
> - keeping a record of the weather
> – observe the signs which tell you it is windy outside, and how strong the wind is
> - clothes we need to wear for different weather conditions
> – sort and group rainy day and sunny day things such as wellingtons, umbrella, sunglasses

> **Experimenting**
> - fabrics that are suitable to wear on wet and dry days
> – test out various fabrics to find if they are waterproof
> - ways in which wet things can dry
> – explore the best days for drying clothes outside
> – observe puddles in the playground and how long they take to dry
> – observe water levels in containers going down over time

> **Solving practical problems**
> - preventing ice forming on a path
> – investigate what can be put on a path to prevent ice forming or help it melt

Handling information

Recording findings

Encourage the children to think about ways in which their findings can be recorded.

Talk with the children about your reasons for choosing a particular method of recording.

Findings from practical problem-solving activities can be recorded through drawing and writing.

Findings from surveys and experiments can be recorded individually or as a group by:
- using simple charts and pictograms
- using tables and bar charts

In the Classroom

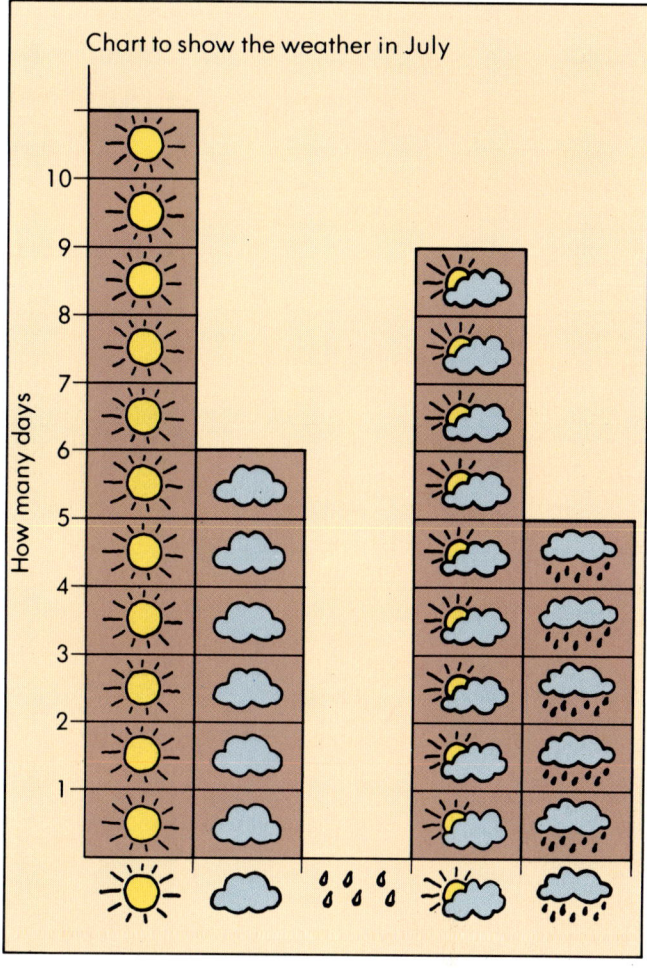

Interpreting findings
Encourage children to link findings and observations, and thus try to establish and express cause-and-effect relationships.

Help the children to link weather conditions to the time of the year, and the time of the year to the pattern of their own day.

Review points
The following are useful talking points:

Our investigations
- the questions we asked
- how we planned
- how we collected information
- how and why we recorded
- what we found out

Making connections
- people whose **occupations** are affected by weather conditions; for example, farmers, pilots and oil-rig workers

125

In the Classroom

Safety

Ensure that the children:

- do not look directly at the sun

Investigations

I wonder whether . . .

- **the clouds look the same every day?**

By observing the clouds in a systematic way and **recording** their observations, the children can gather information about different types of cloud and begin to relate these to different weather conditions.

In the Classroom

- **the wind blows from the same direction every day?**

The children can **observe** the clouds, trees, litter blowing around and washing hanging on lines.

They could **construct** a wind sock or weather vane which would give them more accurate information about wind direction. A wind sock can be made using a tube of fabric or a sleeve from a shirt or blouse. One end of the tube is attached to a wire hoop which is fixed to a pole.

- **when it rains or snows, the same amount falls every day?**

Children can **construct** a rain gauge to **measure** the amount of rain or snow which falls. They could use a capacity container or adapt a plastic lemonade bottle by cutting it across the centre and inverting the neck of the bottle to act as a funnel.

- **we always need to wear extra clothes when we are outside?**

The children can **discuss** the clothes that they wear at different times of the year.

In the Classroom

They could **conduct a survey** about which days they need to wear coats, wellingtons, hats and gloves.

- **we eat different food at different times of the year?**

The children can **discuss** how the weather influences the food that they eat.

They could **cook and prepare** food associated with different seasons; for example, salad, soup, ice cream and porridge.

- **some fabrics are warmer than others?**

The children can **observe and discuss** the clothes that they wear and the fabric from which they are made.

They could **test out** the insulating properties of different fabrics by pouring warm water into containers and covering the containers with different fabrics. The children could test the temperature of the water at different times, by touch or by using a thermometer.

What happens if . . .
- **different fabrics get wet?**

By pouring water onto different fabrics the children can **find out** which fabric would make a good waterproof coat.

Can we find a way to . . .
- **stop things sliding on ice?**

The children can **experiment** with different materials attached to blocks of wood.

They could **collect information** about materials which do not slide on ice and materials which do.

They could **find out** which type of shoe sole is best to prevent sliding on ice.

Evaluation Checklist

Unit . . . . Date . . . .

Teaching
Have the children been provided with opportunities to:

- work on questions or problems which they have accepted as their own? ☐
- work on questions or problems which have enabled them to:

AT9   – observe and talk about the changes in the weather? ☐

AT9   – keep a record of the changes in the weather? ☐

AT9   – talk about ways in which the weather affects their everyday activities? ☐

AT16   – observe and talk about seasonal changes in the weather? ☐

Has the work pupils were engaged in allowed them to:

AT1   • talk about the purposes of recording results? ☐

AT1   • record results by drawing pictures, drawing block graphs and completing frequency charts, tables and bar charts? ☐

AT1   • sort and group objects and events, such as:
- fabrics which allow water through and those which do not? ☐
- days when it rains and days when it does not? ☐
- clothes we wear on rainy days and clothes we do not wear then? ☐

AT1   • distinguish between a fair and an unfair test? ☐

AT1   • interpret records of results? ☐

AT1   • describe activities carried out by sequencing the major features? ☐

AT1   • discuss their observations with other children? ☐

AT1   • describe the best way of recording their activities? ☐

AT1   • relate their findings to previous ideas and experiences? ☐

AT1   • reflect upon how their procedures might be improved? ☐

Learning
Have the children demonstrated that they can:

Level 1
AT9   • talk to you about different weather conditions? ☐

AT9   • tell you about the daily changes in the weather? ☐

AT16   • tell you about the seasonal changes that occur in the weather? ☐

AT1   • make observations about the weather and talk about their observations? ☐

Level 2
AT9   • talk to you about some of the effects that the weather has on their lives? ☐

AT9   • draw pictures and charts to show the weather over a period of time? ☐

AT1   • identify simple variables such as wet/dry, hot/cold? ☐

AT1   • ask questions and suggest ideas of the 'how' and 'why' variety? ☐

AT1   • record findings in charts and drawings? ☐

AT1   • list and collate observations? ☐

Level 3
AT9   • give some examples of the effects of weathering on buildings and on the landscape, for example, fading, paint flaking, brickwork crumbling? ☐

AT9   • tell you that the wind is moving air and that air is all around us? ☐

AT1   • formulate hypotheses? ☐

AT1   • distinguish between a fair and an unfair test? ☐

AT1   • record findings in tables and bar charts? ☐

AT1   • describe activities carried out by sequencing the major features? ☐

Bishop Grosseteste College 1990. Copying permitted for purchasing school only. This material is not 'copyright free'.

SKY AND WEATHER

UNIT 15
CHANGES IN THE SKY: LIGHT AND DARK

Opportunities for learning

The range of suggestions in this unit provides children with the following opportunities from the **programme of study** for key stage 1:

- to explore the effects of the position of the sun in the sky and the length of the day
- to develop their investigative skills and understanding of science in the context of explorations and investigations

The suggestions for practical activities and discussion outlined in this unit provide children with the experiences necessary to facilitate attainment up to level 3.

Topics

Many topics provide children with opportunities for finding out about changes in the sky: light and dark. Some examples are:

TIME	Changes in day length
THE SEASONS	Changes in day length
LIGHT AND DARK	The sun in the sky The moon in the sky Shadows

The flow-diagram in section 1 (figure 3, pp.4–5) will help you identify further topics.

Classroom materials

The following Nelson Science materials support this unit:

Picture Resource Book 1

- p.12 – short shadows
- p.13 – long shadows
- p.14 – position of the sun in the sky
- p.15 – night sky
- p.16 earth, moon and sun

Science Discussion Books for key stage 1

- finding out about sky and weather

Science Explorers

- **Science Explorer, Carrying Out Surveys 1**
- **Science Explorer, Problem Solving 1**

Planning and Preparation

Related units
Children may ask questions which will provide opportunities for finding out about the content of other units. For example:

- light, shadows, colours and mirrors – unit 1
- changes in the weather and the effect of the weather – unit 14

Resources and equipment
- a sundial or construction material to make a sundial such as wood, cord and glue
- a video of any programme which shows the night sky

In the Classroom

Getting started

Starting points
Work on changes in the sky – light and dark – can arise from:

children talking about:
- what they can see in the sky during the day
- what they can see in the sky at night
- bed-time when it is light and when it is dark
- their shadows

children visiting:
- a planetarium

children watching a television programme about:
- the changes in the sky during a 24-hour period

Asking questions
The activities outlined above could lead to questions such as:

I wonder whether . . .
- the sun looks to be in the same position in the sky at different times during the day?
- the sunniest place in the classroom or playground during the morning is the sunniest place during the afternoon?
- shadow lengths change during the day?
- shadow lengths change during the year?
- the sky stays light for the same amount of time each day during the year?

Can we find a way to . . .
- chart the apparent movement of the sun?
- construct a sundial?

Gathering information
Encourage children to think of ways of **gathering information** to help answer the questions.

Investigations which might follow these questions are outlined on pp. 134–136.

Ideas for taking these investigations further are given below.

Further investigations

Carrying out surveys
Collecting information about:
- changes in day length during the year
- talk about the time of year when it gets dark early
- the shape of the moon at different times of the month
- record days when the moon may be seen in the morning

Solving practical problems
- using the position of the sun and a shadow to tell which part of the day it is
- make a sundial to measure shadow lengths at different times

Handling information

Recording findings
Encourage the children to think about ways in which their findings can be recorded.

The Sun sets at night time. In the morning the Sun comes out and the sun is yellow

In the Classroom

Talk with the children about your reasons for choosing a particular method of recording.

Findings from practical problem-solving activities can be recorded through drawing and writing.

Findings from surveys and experiments can be recorded individually or as a group by:

- using simple charts and pictograms
- using tables and bar charts

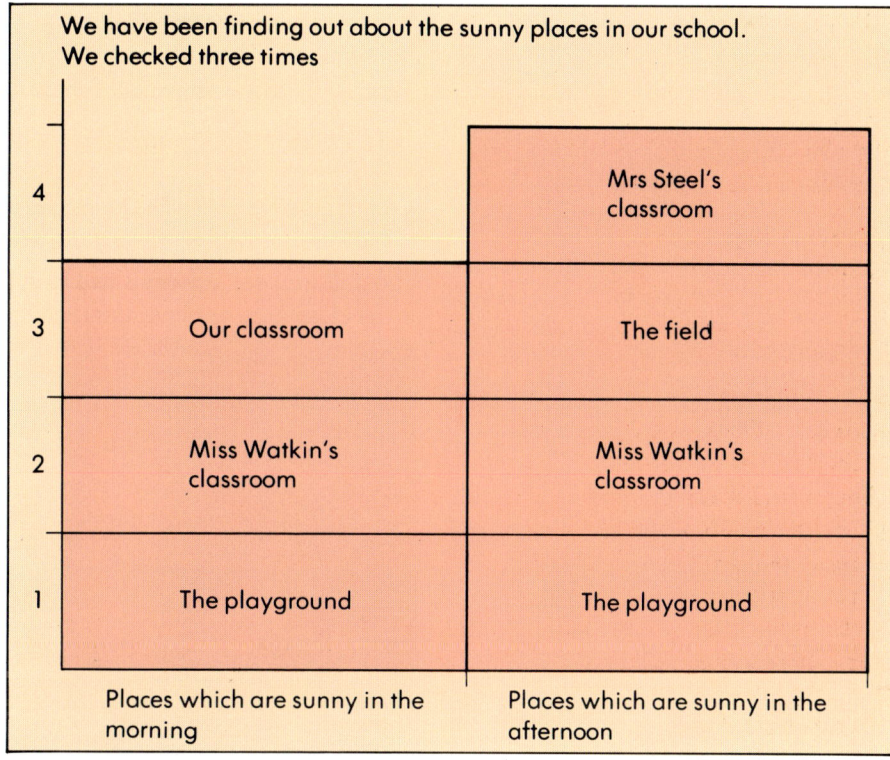

Interpreting findings

Encourage children to link findings and observations, and thus try to establish and express cause-and-effect relationships.

Help children to link the length and position of a shadow with the position of the sun in the sky.

Review points

The following are useful talking points:

Our investigations

- the questions we asked
- how we planned
- how we collected information
- how and why we recorded
- what we found out

Making connections

- the shape of the **earth** and the movement of the earth
- the shape of the **moon** and how the shape that we can see changes

In the Classroom

Safety

Ensure that the children:

- do not look directly at the sun, even through dark glass or plastic

Investigations
I wonder whether . . .

- **the sun looks to be in the same position in the sky at different times during the day?**

The children can **observe** the position of the sun in relation to a tree or building.

They could **draw pictures** to show the position of the sun.

They could **mark** the position, noting the apparent movement of the sun on the classroom window.

- **the sunniest place in the classroom or playground during the morning is the sunniest place during the afternoon?**

The children can **observe and talk about** the way in which the sunniest places in the classroom or playground change during the day.

They could **discuss** which parts of the school get the sun during the morning and afternoon.

- **shadow lengths change during the day?**

The children can **keep a record** of how their own shadow changes in position and length during the day.

They could also use a stick or pole and mark and measure the shadow during the day.

In the Classroom

- **shadow lengths change during the year?**

Children can **keep a record** of the size of their own shadows at different times of the year, such as summer and autumn. (N.B. They will have to keep the time of day the same.)

- **the sky stays light for the same amount of time each day during the year?**

Children can **talk about** their day. They can discuss what sort of things do they do in a day, and whether it is dark or light at bed-time at different times of the year.

Children could **talk about** why they think we have daylight and why it is dark at night.

In the Classroom

Can we find a way to . . .

- **chart the apparent movement of the sun?**

The children can observe where they see the sun in the morning, afternoon and evening.

They could decide through **discussion** the best way to **chart and record** the apparent movement. They could: draw pictures, construct graphs about shadow lengths, mark the position of shadows, or mark the position of the sun on a classroom window.

- **construct a sundial?**

Children can **make** a simple sundial by putting a stick or pole into the ground and marking the position of the shadow at different stages of the day.

Children may want to **construct** a more permanent sundial on a solid base.

Evaluation Checklist

Unit . . . .   Date . . . .

Teaching

Have the children been provided with opportunities to:

- work on questions or problems which they have accepted as their own? ☐
- AT16 • work on questions or problems which have enabled them to:
  - observe and talk about the length of the day? ☐
  - observe and talk about the position of the sun in the sky? ☐
  - observe and talk about the position and shape of the moon in the sky? ☐
  - investigate and talk about the passage of time by using a sundial? ☐

Has the work pupils were engaged in allowed them to:

- AT1 • talk about the purposes of recording results? ☐
- AT1 • record results by drawing pictures, block graphs and bar charts? ☐
- AT1 • sort and group objects and events, such as:
  - days when the sun is visible in the sky and days when it is not? ☐
- AT1 • measure results using non-standard and simple standard measuring skills; for instance, the length of the shadow of a stick? ☐
- AT1 • interpret findings by linking variables? ☐
- AT1 • discuss their observations and ideas with other children? ☐
- AT1 • describe the best way of recording their activities? ☐
- AT1 • relate their findings to previous ideas and experiences? ☐
- AT1 • reflect upon how their procedures might be improved? ☐

Learning

Have the children demonstrated that they can:

Level 1
- AT16 • talk about the apparent daily motion of the sun across the sky in relation to their home or school? ☐
- AT1 • make observations about the sun, the moon and shadows and talk about their observations? ☐

Level 2
- AT16 • talk about why night occurs? ☐
- AT16 • tell you about daylight hours getting longer or shorter during the year? ☐
- AT16 • tell you that the earth is a large, spherical, self-contained planet? ☐
- AT16 • talk about and draw pictures to show that the earth, moon and sun are separate bodies? ☐
- AT1 • identify simple variables such as light/dark, day/night? ☐
- AT1 • ask questions and suggest ideas of the 'how' and 'why' variety? ☐
- AT1 • measure using non-standard and standard units? ☐
- AT1 • record findings in charts and drawings? ☐
- AT1 • list and collate observations? ☐
- AT1 • interpret findings by associating one factor with another, such as the position of the sun affecting shadow? ☐

Level 3
- AT16 • tell you about the sun being higher in the sky in the summer than the winter? ☐
- AT1 • formulate hypotheses? ☐
- AT1 • distinguish between a fair and an unfair test? ☐
- AT1 • measure using simple measuring instruments, such as a ruler, to the nearest labelled division? ☐
- AT1 • record your findings in tables and bar charts? ☐
- AT1 • describe activities carried out by sequencing the major features ☐
- AT1 • interpret findings in terms of a generalised statement, such as 'the higher the position of the sun in the sky the shorter the shadow'? ☐

Bishop Grosseteste College 1990. Copying permitted for purchasing school only. This material is not 'copyright free'.

SKY AND WEATHER

UNIT 16
CHANGES IN TEMPERATURE: HOT AND COLD

Opportunities for learning

The range of suggestions in this unit provides children with the following opportunities from the **programme of study** for key stage 1:

- to explore the effect of heating and cooling water and ice and to link the feeling of hot and cold with temperature measured by a thermometer
- to develop their investigative skills and understanding of science in the context of explorations and investigations

    The suggestions for practical activities and discussion outlined in this unit provide children with the experiences necessary to facilitate attainment up to level 3.

Topics

Many topics provide children with opportunities for finding out about changes in temperature: hot and cold. Some examples are:

WEATHER	Changes in temperature Snow and ice
HOT AND COLD	Effects of heating and cooling water
OURSELVES	Keeping warm and cool Comparing things that are hot and cold relative to their own bodies

The flow-diagram in section 1 (figure 3, pp.4–5) will help you identify further topics.

Classroom materials

The following Nelson Science materials support this unit:

Picture Resource Book 1

- p.4 – cacti
- p.20 – cold climates
- p.21 – desert conditions
- p.22 – tropical climates

Science Discussion Books for key stage 1

- finding out about sky and weather

Science Explorers

- **Science Explorer, Carrying Out Surveys 1**
- **Science Explorer, Experimenting 1**
- **Science Explorer, Problem Solving 1**

Planning and Preparation

Related units

Children may ask questions which will provide opportunities for finding out about the content of other units. For example:

- changes in the weather and the effect of the weather – unit 14
- everyday substances which melt and solidify: ice/water, wax, chocolate etc. – unit 19

Resources and equipment

- a range of containers of different shapes and sizes, such as jugs and bowls
- a range of fabrics such as wool, nylon and cotton
- ice cubes or an ice block
- access to a refrigerator with a freezing compartment

In the Classroom

Getting started

Starting points
Work on changes in temperature, hot and cold, can arise from:

children talking about:
- the snow in winter
- ways of keeping warm
- using ice in drinks
- ways of keeping drinks warm

children making:
- ice lollies

Asking questions
The activities outlined above could lead to questions such as:

I wonder whether . . .
- some things feel colder or warmer than others?
- the snow will melt today?

What happens if . . .
- snow or ice is put in different places around the classroom?
- water is put into different shaped containers and put into the freezer?
- ice is put into cold water?
- ice is put into warm water?

Can we find a way to . . .
- prevent ice cubes from melting?
- find the coldest or warmest part of the room?

Gathering information
Encourage children to think of ways of **gathering information** to help answer the questions.

Investigations which might follow these questions are outlined on pp. 141–143.

Ideas for taking these investigations further are given below.

Further investigations

Carrying out surveys
Collecting information about:
- the temperature of their own bodies
  – explore whether some parts of their bodies are warmer than others
- the temperature of different areas of the school
  – use a thermometer to measure the temperature

Experimenting
- keeping ice or snow in the classroom
  – time the rate of thaw
- observing the effect of freezing different quantities of water

Solving practical problems
- preventing water in pipes from freezing
  – use a variety of materials to lag out-of-doors pipes or containers

Handling information

Recording findings
Encourage the children to think about ways in which their findings can be recorded.

Talk with the children about your reasons for choosing a particular method of recording.

Findings from practical problem-solving activities can be recorded through drawing and writing.

In the Classroom

Findings from surveys and experiments can be recorded individually or as a group by:
- using simple charts and pictograms
- using tables and bar charts

Interpreting findings
Encourage children to link findings and observations, and thus try to establish and express cause-and-effect relationships – for example, between temperature and melting; between the reading on the thermometer and how hot or cold something feels.

Review points
The following are useful talking points:

Our investigations
- the questions we asked
- how we planned
- how we collected information
- how and why we recorded
- what we found out

Making connections
- people who **use thermometers in their occupations**; for example, nurses, doctors, gardeners, meteorologists

Safety
Ensure that the children:
- use only safe, non mercury thermometers
- do no handle hot water
- do not put hot water into glass containers

Investigations

I wonder whether . . .
- some things feel colder or warmer than others?

The children can conduct surveys both inside and outside the classroom.

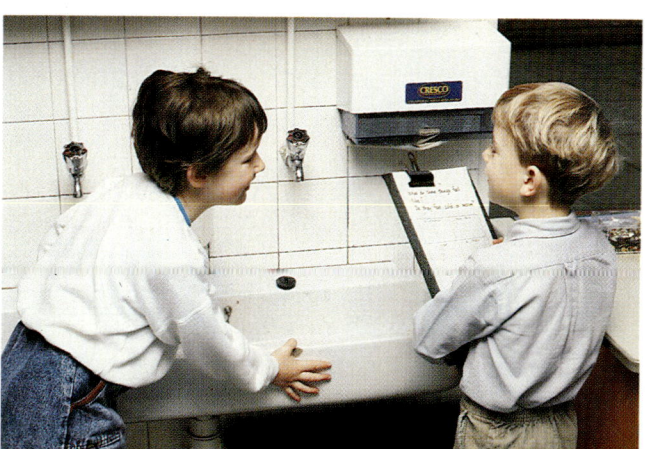

In the Classroom

They could observe and find out if some materials feel warmer to the touch than others.

They could sort and group materials and areas of the buildings into sets of things which feel warm and those which do not.

- **the snow will melt today?**

By observing the sky and consciously noticing how warm the sun or the air temperature feels, the children could predict whether or not the snow will melt.

They could discuss which weather conditions make snow and which cause snow to melt.

What happens if . . .
- **snow or ice is put in different places around the classroom?**

In the Classroom

The children can predict in which places the snow or ice will melt or will last longest.

They could decide on how they could make it a fair test by controlling the amount of ice or snow and deciding on the containers they would use.

- **water is put into different shaped containers and put into the freezer?**

The children can predict how long it will take for the water to turn into ice.

They could **find out** whether the water in the different shaped containers will take different times.

They could **investigate** how to get the ice out of the containers.

- **ice is put into cold water?**
- **ice is put into warm water?**

The children can **predict** and then **collect information** about the rate of thaw when ice is put into cold or warm water.

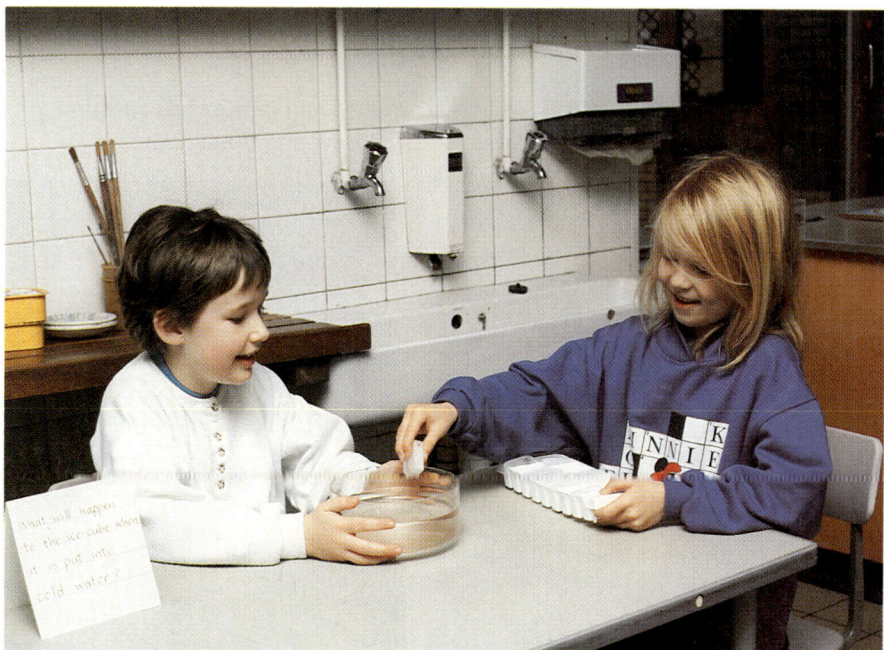

In the Classroom

They could use different amounts of ice to find out whether the size of the ice cube or block influences the results.

Can we find a way to . . .

- **prevent ice cubes from melting?**

The children can put ice cubes into containers such as jugs and bowls, and put them in different places around the classroom.

They could cover the containers with materials such as cooking foil or different fabrics such as wool, nylon and cotton.

They could put ice cubes into a thermos flask and **record** how long the ice cubes remain.

- **find the coldest or warmest part of the room?**

The children can **use their sense of touch**, or place a thermometer in different areas of the classroom.

They could **find out** if there are parts of the classroom which are colder or warmer than others.

They could **gather information** about the temperature of the air around windows and open doors.

Evaluation Checklist

Unit .... Date ....

Teaching
Have the children been provided with opportunities to:

- work on questions or problems which they have accepted as their own? ☐

AT13
- work on questions or problems which have enabled them to:
  - explore the effect of heating water and ice? ☐
  - explore and investigate how ice melts? ☐
  - explore and investigate how water freezes? ☐
  - link the feeling of hot and cold with temperature measured by a thermometer? ☐
  - measure temperature with a thermometer? ☐

Has the work pupils were engaged in allowed them to:

- AT1 • talk to you about the purposes of recording results? ☐
- AT1 • record results by drawing pictures, block graphs and bar charts? ☐
- AT1 • sort and group objects and events, such as:
  - places in the classroom which are warm and those which are not? ☐
  - objects which feel warm to the touch and those which do not? ☐
- AT1 • distinguish between a fair and an unfair test? ☐
- AT1 • interpret findings by linking variables? ☐
- AT1 • describe activities carried out by sequencing the major features? ☐
- AT1 • discuss their observations with other children? ☐
- AT1 • describe the best way of recording their activities? ☐
- AT1 • relate their findings to previous ideas and experiences? ☐
- AT1 • reflect upon how their procedures might be improved? ☐

Learning
Have the children demonstrated that they can:

Level 1
- AT1 • make observations about hot things and cold things and talk about their observations? ☐

Level 2
- AT13 • tell you if objects feel hot or cold to their touch? ☐
- AT13 • talk to you about how hot or cold their bodies feel when they are in different places? ☐
- AT1 • identify simple variables such as hot/cold? ☐
- AT1 • ask questions and suggest ideas of the 'how' and 'why' variety? ☐
- AT1 • record findings in charts and drawings? ☐
- AT1 • list and collate observations? ☐
- AT13 • measure temperature with a thermometer? ☐
- AT13 • read a thermometer to tell you how hot or cold things are? ☐
- AT1 • formulate hypotheses? ☐
- AT1 • distinguish between a fair and an unfair test? ☐
- AT1 • record findings in tables and bar charts? ☐
- AT1 • describe activities carried out by sequencing the major features? ☐

Bishop Grosseteste College 1990. Copying permitted for purchasing school only. This material is not 'copyright free'.

MOVING THINGS

UNIT 17
HOW TO MAKE THINGS MOVE

Opportunities for learning

The range of suggestions in this unit provides children with the following opportunities from the **programme of study** for key stage 1:

- to explore the forces which make things move and stop things from moving
- to explore devices which move and store energy
- to develop their investigative skills and understanding of science in the context of explorations and investigations

The suggestions for practical activities and discussion outlined in this unit provide children with the experiences necessary to facilitate attainment up to level 3.

Topics

Many topics provide children with opportunities for finding out about how to make things move. Some examples are:

TOYS	Movement of toys Movement of clockwork toys Movement of battery-powered toys
OURSELVES	Ways in which we move
THE PLAYPARK AND THE FUNFAIR	Movement of the rides Swings, roundabouts, slides and see-saws
ROAD SAFETY	How vehicles stop Speed of vehicles
THE WEATHER	Wind power

The flow-diagram in section 1 (figure 3, pp.4–5) will help you identify further topics.

Classroom materials

The following Nelson Science materials support this unit:

Science Discussion Books for key stage 1

- finding out about moving things

Science Explorers

- Science Explorer, Carrying Out Surveys 1
- Science Explorer, Experimenting 1
- Science Explorer, Problem Solving 1

The Picture Resource Books do not contain material to cover this unit, because children's learning about moving things will develop through practical activity alone.

Planning and preparation

Related units

Children may ask questions which will provide opportunities for finding out about the content of other units. For example:

- growing and moving – unit 5
- changes in the weather and the effect of the weather – unit 14
- using materials to make structures – unit 21

Resources and equipment

- a range of wheeled toys
- batteries and simple motors
- Lego vehicles
- bricks (toy or full size)
- a ramp
- different types of material to cover the ramp, such as lino, carpet, sandpaper, plastic sheeting
- a pulley
- string
- plasticine
- wheels of different sizes

In the Classroom

Getting started

Starting points
Work on how to make things move can arise from:

children talking about:
- their toys
- a windy day
- road safety

children having visits from:
- the police
- the lollipop lady/man

children being involved in:
- water play
- construction play
- outdoor play activities with: kites, the climbing frame, swings and slides

children making collections of:
- toys which move in different ways, such as vehicles, yo-yos, clockwork toys and spinning tops

Asking questions
The activities outlined above could lead to questions such as:

I wonder whether . . .
- the wind can make things move?
- some toy cars move further than others?
- some toy cars move faster than others?
- some things sink and some things float in water?

What happens if . . .
- we sit in pairs facing each other and push and pull with our hands?
- a toy car is put on a ramp?

Can we find a way to . . .
- move a weight across a surface?
- move a toy car up a ramp?
- make a cotton-reel tank?
- make a boat that floats?

Gathering information
Encourage children to think of ways of **gathering information** to help answer these questions.

Investigations which might follow these questions are outlined on pp. 149–152.
Ideas for taking these investigations further are given below.

Further investigations

Carrying out surveys
Collecting information about:
- the forces that make things move
– compare the movement of trees and litter on windy days and calm days
– observe how the rain makes leave move
– use straws, pipes, tubing and squeezy bottles to make water move
- the movement of play-park equipment
– observe how a swing moves
– observe what movement starts a swing
– investigate how a see-saw moves
– investigate how people balance on a see-saw

Experimenting
- making toys move faster and slower
– observe the movement of toys
– give different amounts of energy to a toy; for example, bigger push, new battery, extra turns on the key

Solving practical problems
- road safety activities
– investigate how to make a toy car stop at a certain place
- constructing a toy
– make a toy which rolls
– make a toy which balances
– make a kite that will fly on a windy day

Handling information

Recording findings
Encourage the children to think about ways in which their findings can be recorded.

Talk with the children about your reasons for choosing a particular method of recording.

Findings from practical problem-solving activities can be recorded through drawing and writing.

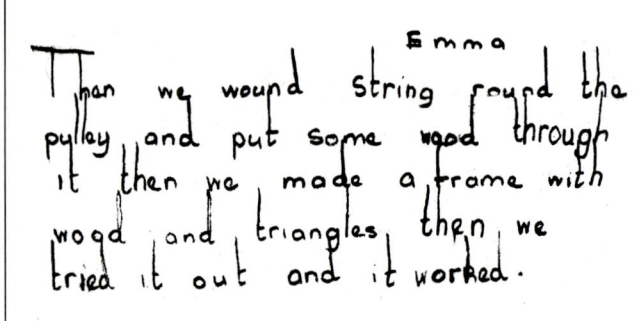

In the Classroom

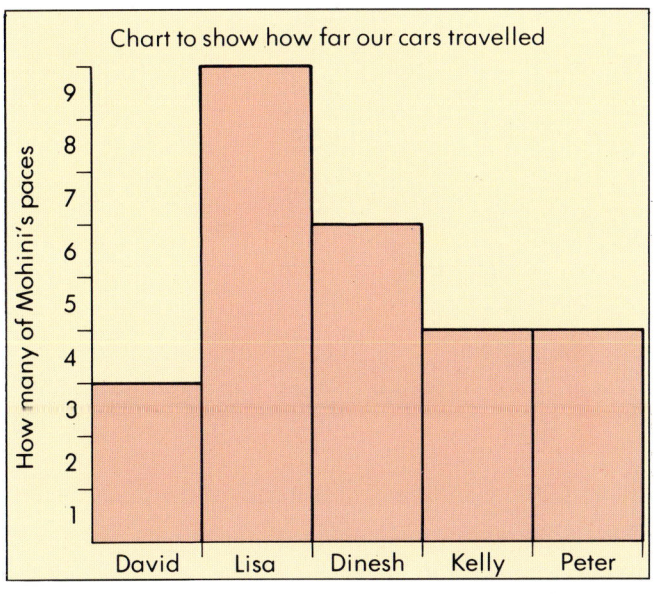

Findings from surveys and experiments can be recorded individually or as a group by:
- using simple charts and pictograms
- using tables and bar charts

Interpreting findings

Encourage children to link findings and observations, and thus try to establish and express cause-and-effect relationships – for example, between the height of a ramp and how far a toy car travels.

Review points

The following are useful talking points:

Our investigations
- the questions we asked
- how we planned
- how we collected information
- how and why we recorded
- what we found out

Making connections
- the things in the **home or classroom** which require pulls, pushes and turns; for example, opening a door, closing a drawer, turning on a tap
- the need for safe and careful action when **crossing the road**

Safety

Ensure that the children:
- are carefully monitored during any investigation which requires them to drop objects

Investigations

I wonder whether . . .
- **the wind can make things move?**

The children can observe and list the things that the wind moves, such as leaves, litter, washing, flags.

149

In the Classroom

From these initial observations they could set up fair tests by trying to move:
- a boat with a sail across the water trough
- a wheeled car
- a piece of paper

They could waft a newspaper behind these things, or use a hair dryer, or they could blow.

- some toy cars move further than others?
- some toy cars move faster than others?

The children could **collect** a number of different toy cars.

They could **sort and group** them into sets of battery powered cars, clockwork or wind-up cars, or cars which need a push to make them go.

They could **collect information** about cars which travel further or faster than others and talk about how these cars move.

- **some things sink and some things float?**

The children could **make a collection** of everyday objects of different materials.

They could **predict** which things would sink or float.

They could **sort, group and order** the objects according to whether they floated well or sunk.

What happens if...

- **we sit in pairs facing each other and push and pull with our hands?**

By moving in this way the children can experience the force of their body behind pushing and pulling movements.

They could **talk about** which parts of their body are moving when they move in this way.

In the Classroom

- **a toy car is put on a ramp?**

The children can measure how far a car travels down a ramp supported by one brick.

They could increase the number of bricks and collect information about the distance the car travels.

They could discuss why the results appear different when more than one brick is used.

Can we find a way to . . .

- **move a weight across a surface?**

The children could talk about and devise a way of moving a heavy object such as a brick across a surface.

They could **find out** if it would slide down a ramp.

They could put different shapes underneath and try to push it across the shapes.

They could pull it across the surface by putting paper or fabric underneath.

- **move a toy car up a ramp?**

By using a simple pulley device the children could experiment with pulling a toy car up a ramp.

They could attach a length of string to the car, place weights on the end of the string and hang the weights over the edge of the ramp. The children could **collect information** about how much weight was needed to pull the car up certain distances.

- **make a cotton reel tank?**

Children can thread an elastic band through a cotton reel and put a small piece of dowel or a used match-stick through each loop of the elastic band. By twisting the elastic band the children can get the cotton reel to travel.

In the Classroom

They could gather information about the relationship between the number of twists of the elastic band and how far the cotton-reel tank travels.

- **make a boat that floats?**

The children can **change the shape** of an object in order to make it float.

They could make a boat from plasticine or paper.

They could explore how to get their boat to travel as far as possible.

Evaluation Checklist

Unit . . . . Date . . . .

Teaching
Have the children been provided with opportunities to:

- work on questions or problems which they have accepted as their own? ☐
- work on questions or problems which have enabled them to:

AT10 — be involved in play activities in order to explore the forces which make things move, stop things and change the shape of objects? ☐

AT13 — explore and talk about how toys and other devices move and store energy? ☐

Has the work pupils were engaged in allowed them to:

AT1 • talk about the purposes of recording results? ☐

AT1 • record results by drawing pictures, drawing block graphs and completing tables and bar charts? ☐

AT1 • sort and group objects, such as:
  – toys which will move with a push and those which will not? ☐
  – toys which have wheels and those which do not? ☐
  – objects which change shape when they are dropped and those which do not? ☐

AT1 • measure using non-standard and simple standard measuring skills; for example, how far they can get a toy car to travel? ☐

AT1 • distinguish between a fair and un unfair test; for example, starting the car at the same place on the ramp to test how far it travels each time? ☐

AT1 • interpret findings by linking variables? ☐

AT1 • describe activities carried out by sequencing the major features? ☐

AT1 • discuss their observations and ideas with other children? ☐

AT1 • describe the best way of recording their activities? ☐

AT1 • relate their findings to previous ideas and experiences? ☐

AT1 • reflect upon how their procedures might be improved? ☐

Learning
Have the children demonstrated that they can:

Level 1
AT1 • make observations of things moving and stopping and talk about their observations? ☐

Level 2
AT10 • tell you how they can make things start moving, speed up, swerve or stop through pushes and pulls? ☐

AT13 • tell you how a wind-up or clockwork toy works? ☐

AT1 • identify simple variables such as fast/slow? ☐

AT1 • ask questions and suggest ideas of the 'how' and 'why' variety? ☐

AT1 • measure using non-standard and standard units? ☐

AT1 • record findings in charts and drawings? ☐

AT1 • list and collate observations? ☐

AT1 • interpret findings by associating one factor with another, such as the 'weight' of objects and their ability to float? ☐

Level 3
AT10 • tell you why things change shape, begin to move or stop moving? ☐

AT10 • talk to you about the factors which cause objects to float or sink in water? ☐

AT13 • tell you about some of the ways in which they can make a model or machine work? ☐

AT13 • talk to you about power sources, such as electric motors and rubber bands, and devices such as gears, belts and levers which they have used to make models and machines work? ☐

AT1 • formulate hypotheses? ☐

AT1 • distinguish between a fair and an unfair test? ☐

AT1 • measure using simple measuring instruments, such as a ruler, to the nearest labelled division? ☐

AT1 • record findings in tables and bar charts? ☐

AT1 • describe activities carried out by sequencing the major features? ☐

AT1 • interpret findings in terms of a generalised statement, for example, 'the harder the push the further the vehicle will travel'; 'the harder the push the higher the swing will go'? ☐

Bishop Grosseteste College 1990. Copying permitted for purchasing school only. This material is not 'copyright free'.

MATERIALS

UNIT 18
NATURAL MATERIALS FOUND IN THE LOCALITY: STONES, ROCKS, SOIL

Opportunities for learning

The range of suggestions in this unit provides children with the following opportunities from the **programme of study** for key stage 1:

- to explore the properties of locally found natural materials
- to use simple processes to change some of these materials
- to develop their investigative skills and understanding of science in the context of explorations and investigations

The suggestions for practical activities and discussion outlined in this unit provide children with the experiences necessary to facilitate attainment up to level 3.

Topics

Many topics provide children with opportunities for finding out about natural materials found in the locality: stones, rocks, soil. Some examples are:

MINIBEASTS	Soil types Wet and dry soil conditions
PLANTS	Soil types Content of soil
BUILDINGS	Stone as a building material Strength of stone
THE SEASIDE	Sorting and grouping pebbles Looking closely at sand

The flow-diagram in section 1 (figure 3, pp.4–5) will help you identify further topics.

Classroom materials

The following Nelson Science materials support this unit:

Picture Resource Book 3

- p.5 – origins of clay
- p.6 – origins of coal
- p.7 – origins of chalk
- p.8 – folding of rocks
- p.9 – effects of weathering

Science Discussion Books for key stage 1

- finding out about materials

Planning and Preparation

Science Explorers
- **Science Explorer, Carrying Out Surveys 1**
- **Science Explorer, Experimenting 1**
- **Science Explorer, Problem Solving 1**

Related units

Children may ask questions which will provide opportunities for finding out about the content of other units. For example:

- improving the appearance of the local environment – unit 4
- how to take care of plants – unit 8
- everyday materials: sand, wood, metal, plastics, paper, clay, fabrics, (including magnets) – unit 20

Resources and equipment

- a variety of different stones and rocks including those found in the immediate locality and any additional rocks, such as limestone, chalk, granite and sandstone, which are found in other localities
- soil samples from the immediate locality
- an augur
- collecting containers
- a small trowel

In the Classroom

Getting started

Starting points
Work on natural materials found in the locality, stones, rocks, soil, can arise from:

children visiting:
- a quarry
- a mine
- a museum
- the seaside

children making collections of:
- stones and pebbles of different colours, sizes and shapes
- rocks
- wood

children creating:
- a school garden
- a habitat for animals or plants

Asking questions
The activities outlined above could lead to questions such as:

I wonder whether...
- all rocks are the same colour?
- all rocks are the same shape?
- some rocks sparkle?
- soil feels gritty, silky or smooth?
- soil samples are the same all the way down?

What happens if...
- water is poured onto rocks?
- rocks are scratched?
- a soil sample is shaken in a jar of water and then left to settle?
- soil is sifted through a sieve?

Can we find a way to...
- make a clay model hard?
- make hard clay soft again?
- roll soil into a sausage shape?

Gathering information
Encourage children to think of ways of **gathering information** to help answer these questions.

Investigations which might follow these questions are outlined on pp. 157–160.

Ideas for taking these investigations further are given below.

Further investigations

Carrying out surveys

Collecting information about:
- soil samples
– collect and compare soil found in different areas around the school
– make observations about and record the content of soil; for example, stones, leaves, roots

Experimenting
- changing the consistency of soil
– make observations and record the changes when water, sand or peat (compost) is added to soil

Solving practical problems
- creating a garden area
– investigate the best soil for growing plants
– cultivate part of the school ground and grow flowers and vegetables

Handling information

Recording findings
Encourage the children to think about ways in which their findings can be recorded.

Talk with the children about your reasons for choosing a particular method of recording.

Findings from practical problem-solving activities can be recorded through drawing and writing.

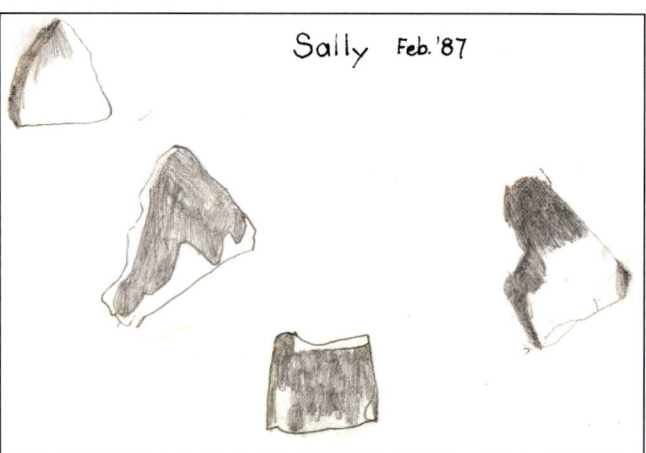

Findings from surveys and experiments can be recorded individually or as a group by:
- using simple charts and pictograms
- using tables and bar charts

In the Classroom

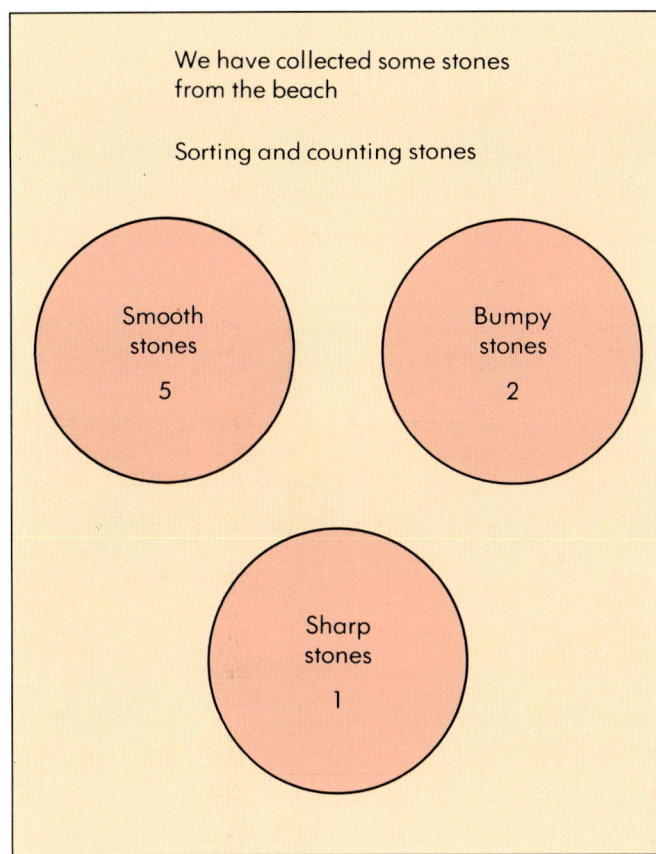

We have collected some stones from the beach

Sorting and counting stones

- Smooth stones 5
- Bumpy stones 2
- Sharp stones 1

Interpreting findings

Encourage children to link findings and observations, and thus try to establish and express cause-and-effect relationships.

Help the children to link characteristics, such as whether rocks and stones crumble or will scratch other surfaces, to the idea of hardness.

Review points

The following are useful talking points:

Our investigations
- the questions we asked
- how we planned
- how we collected information
- how and why we recorded
- what we found out

Making connections
- how **different localities** may have different stones, rocks and soil formation
- the **seaside and desert**
- how **humans have used natural materials**, such as flint and iron for tools, peat and wood for fuel, and stones and wood for building

Safety

Ensure that the children:
- always wash their hands thoroughly after they have handled soil and before touching things to be put into their mouths

Investigations
I wonder whether...
- all rocks are the same colour?
- all rocks are the same shape?
- some rocks sparkle?

The children can **collect** a wide variety of rocks, stones and pebbles.

Through **observation, sorting and grouping** activities the children can begin to **collect information** about the different rocks found in one area.

They might begin to **ask questions** about how the rocks got there.

In the Classroom

- **soil feels gritty, silky or smooth?**

The children can be encouraged to handle soil and to use all of their senses to **make observations**.

They could compare the soil found in the immediate locality with other types of soil; for instance, clay.

- **soil samples are the same all the way down?**

The children can dig through wet or damp soil to collect a soil sample. They could use a trowel or augur to get a clean-cut sample.

They could **make observations** about the content of the sample. They may notice layers of different materials in it.

What happens if . . .

- **water is poured onto rocks?**

The children can **closely observe** what happens.

They could **collect information** about how porous the rock is.

They could **record** any changes in colour, weight or texture of the rock.

- **rocks are scratched?**

The children can **gather information** about the hardness or softness of rocks.

They could **collect information** about rocks which will scratch other rocks.

In the Classroom

- **a soil sample is shaken in a jar of water and then left to settle?**

By **closely observing** what happens the children can begin to gather information about the content of soil and how it separates out in water.

Their attention could be drawn to the fact that some things, like pebbles, sink rapidly to the bottom of the jar while some debris is left floating on the surface. They could observe the colour of the water.

- **soil is sifted through a sieve?**

The children can use a number of sieves to separate the contents of soil.

They could then **sort and order** the contents before **recording** what they have found.

Can we find a way to . . .

- **make a clay model hard?**

The children can handle clay and make simple models.

They could leave the models exposed to air or fire the model in a kiln.

They could weigh or **balance** the clay before and after it is dry, and **record** the information they have gathered.

- **make hard clay soft?**

The children can use their senses to **make observations** about hard clay.

159

In the Classroom

- **roll soil into a sausage shape?**

The children can add water to garden soil and mould it into a ball or sausage shape.

They could leave the soil to dry out and **record** the outcome.

Evaluation Checklist

Unit . . . .   Date . . . .

Teaching
Have the children been provided with opportunities to:

- work on questions or problems which they have accepted as their own? ☐
- work on questions or problems which have enabled them to:

AT6	– collect natural materials such as rocks, stones and soil from their local environment?	☐
AT6	– look for similarities and differences in a variety of natural materials?	☐
AT6	– explore and investigate some of the changes that simple processes, such as dissolving, squashing, pouring, bending, twisting and treating surfaces, can make in materials?	☐
AT9	– collect and talk about natural materials such as rocks, stones and soil found in their local environment?	☐
AT9	– sort and group these materials by looking for similarities and differences in them?	☐
AT9	– compare and contrast locally found materials with those described at second hand?	☐

Has the work pupils were engaged in allowed them to:

AT1	• talk about the purposes of recording results?	☐
AT1	• record results by drawing pictures, drawing block graphs, and completing tables and bar charts?	☐
AT1	• sort and group objects and events, such as:	
	– rocks and stones which have one colour and those which have more than one colour?	☐
	– rocks and stones which are smooth and those which are not?	☐
	– the components from soil samples; for example, stones, animal matter, plant matter, soil?	☐
AT1	• measure using non-standard and simple standard measuring skills; for example, how heavy the rocks are they have found; how many stones balance one rock?	☐
AT1	• distinguish between a fair and an unfair test; for example, making sure the same amount of water is poured onto rocks?	☐
AT1	• interpret findings by linking variables?	☐
AT1	• describe activities carried out by sequencing the major features?	☐
AT1	• discuss their observations and ideas with other children?	☐
AT1	• describe the best way of making a record of their activities?	☐
AT1	• relate their findings to previous ideas and experiences?	☐
AT1	• reflect upon how their procedures might be improved?	☐

Learning
Have the children demonstrated that they can:

Level 1

AT6	• talk to you about the shape, colour and texture of soil, rocks and stones?	☐
AT6	• tell you what happens to rocks, stones and soil when they have been changed by simple processes, such as squashing and treating the surfaces?	☐
AT1	• make observations of natural materials and talk about their observations?	☐

Level 2

AT6	• tell you about the similarities and differences in rocks, stones and soil samples, such as hardness, flexibility and transparency?	☐
AT9	• sort and group materials according to their characteristics?	☐
AT9	• sort and group materials for a number of different criteria?	☐
AT1	• identify simple variables such as shiny/dull, large/small, rough/smooth, soft/hard?	☐
AT1	• ask questions and suggest ideas of the 'how' and 'why' variety?	☐
AT1	• measure using standard and non-standard units?	☐
AT1	• record findings in charts and drawings?	☐
AT1	• list and collate observations?	☐

Level 3

AT6	• give some examples of those materials which occur naturally and those which are made from raw materials?	☐
AT6	• list the similarities and differences in rocks, stones and soil?	☐
AT9	• tell you that different types of local soil are formed from weathered rocks?	☐
AT9	• talk about one of their investigations with rocks or soil?	☐
AT1	• formulate hypotheses?	☐
AT1	• distinguish between a fair and an unfair test?	☐
AT1	• select and use simple instruments to enhance observation, such as a hand lens?	☐
AT1	• record findings in tables and bar charts?	☐
AT1	• describe activities carried out by sequencing the major features?	☐

Bishop Grosseteste College 1990. Copying permitted for purchasing school only. This material is not 'copyright free'.

MATERIALS

UNIT 19
EVERYDAY SUBSTANCES WHICH MELT AND SOLIDIFY: ICE/WATER, WAX, CHOCOLATE ETC.

Opportunities for learning

The range of suggestions in this unit provides children with the following opportunities from the **programme of study** for key stage 1:

- to explore ways of changing a variety of everyday materials by using simple processes such as dissolving, squashing, pouring and cooking
- to explore the effect of heating common, everyday substances
- to develop their investigative skills and understanding of science in the context of explorations and investigations

The suggestions for practical activities and discussion outlines in this unit provide children with the experiences necessary to facilitate attainment up to level 3.

Topics

Many topics provide children with opportunities for finding out about everyday substances which melt and solidify: ice/water, wax, chocolate etc. Some examples are:

THE WEATHER	Ice thawing Chocolate melting Water freezing
THE GINGERBREAD BOY	Cooking and baking
COLOUR	Melting jellies Jelly moulds
WATER	Substances which dissolve in water Making bubbles with water and detergent
FESTIVALS	Candles melting

The flow-diagram in section 1 (figure 3, pp.4–5) will help you identify further topics.

Classroom materials

The following Nelson Science materials support this unit:

Science Discussion Books for key stage 1

- finding out about materials

Planning and Preparation

Science Explorer
- **Science Explorer, Carrying Out Surveys 1**
- **Science Explorer, Experimenting 1**
- **Science Explorer, Problem Solving 1**

Related units
Children may ask questions which will provide opportunities for finding out about the content of other units. For example:
- changes in temperature: hot and cold – unit 16

Resources and equipment
- cookery books
- ingredients for cooking, including chocolate and jelly
- a range of containers, such as bowls and jugs of different sizes and materials
- a thermometer
- access to a refrigerator and a cooker

In the Classroom

Getting started

Starting points
Work on everyday substances which melt and solidify, ice/water, wax, chocolate etc., can arise from:

children playing in:
- the water tray
- the sand tray

children cooking or preparing food such as:
- jelly
- biscuits
- chocolate Easter eggs
- ice lollies

children reading/listening to stories such as:
- 'The Gingerbread Boy'

children visiting:
- a bakery
- a sweet-shop

Asking questions
The activities outlined about could lead to questions such as:

> **I wonder whether . . .**
> - something which has melted can become solid again?

> **What happens if . . .**
> - chocolate, butter or margarine is left in a sunny place?
> - jelly cubes are put into cold water?
> - jelly cubes are put into hot water?

> **Can we find a way to . . .**
> - make a jelly set?
> - make a candle?

Gathering information
Encourage children to think of ways of gathering information to help answer these questions.

Investigations which might follow these questions are outlined on pp. 166–168.

Ideas for taking these investigations further are given below.

Further investigations

> **Carrying out surveys**
> **Collecting information about:**
> - cooking ingredients
> - compare ingredients which melt and dry
> - observe the changes that occur in melted butter or chocolate
> - observe how ingredients which melt are packaged

> **Experimenting**
> - varying the amount of heat needed to melt or solidify substances
> - look for warm and cold places around the classroom or school
> - use a fridge, freezer, cooker or microwave

> **Solving practical problems**
> - preventing chocolate buttons from melting
> - use different wrappers
> - store in different places

Handling information

Recording findings
Encourage the children to think about ways in which their findings can be recorded.

Talk with the children about your reasons for choosing a particular method of recording.

Findings from practical problem-solving activities can be recorded through drawing and writing.

164

In the Classroom

Findings from surveys and experiments can be recorded individually or as a group by:

- using simple charts and pictograms
- using tables and bar charts

Interpreting findings

Encourage children to link findings and observations, and thus try to establish and express cause-and-effect relationships.

Help children to link high temperature with some materials, like chocolate, ice and wax, melting.

Review points

The following are useful talking points:

Our investigations

- the questions we asked
- how we planned
- how we collected information
- how and why we recorded
- what we found out

Making connections

- **recipes** the children have used in school or at home which involved melting and solidifying substances

Safety

Ensure that the children:

- do not handle hot or boiling liquids
- do not touch hot cooking equipment such as ovens, pans or spoons

In the Classroom

Investigations

I wonder whether . . .

- **something which has melted can become solid again?**

The children can **discuss** what happens to butter or chocolate or ice after it has melted.

They could think about ways of making them solid again.

What happens if . . .

- **chocolate, butter or margarine is left in a sunny place?**

The children will probably have had **previous experience** of chocolate melting in their hands or pockets.

They could **predict** what would happen to substances left in different places around the classroom.

They could **discuss** why these substances melt in certain places and **link these observations** with their experiences of cooking with chocolate and butter.

- **jelly cubes are put into cold water?**

The children can **predict** the outcome and then **record** their findings.

In the Classroom

- **jelly cubes are put into hot water?**

The children can **use their observations** to talk about what happens when jelly is put into cold and hot water.

They could talk about the role of heat in helping the jelly to melt.

Can we find a way to . . .

- **make a jelly set?**

The children will have had **previous experience** of making jelly. They could discuss the best way of making the jelly set.

They could **gather information** about whether jellies set faster in a warm place, a cool place or a refrigerator, or with less water added to them.

In the Classroom

- **make a candle?**

Children can **observe** a candle burning.

They could **talk about** what happens to the wax and why they think the wax is melting.

They could extinguish the candle and **gather information** about how long it takes the wax to harden.

The children could **talk about and plan** ways of making their own candles, either by layering melted wax onto a candle wick, or pouring it into suitable containers.

Evaluation Checklist

Unit .... Date ....

Teaching
Have the children been provided with opportunities to:

- work on questions or problems which they have accepted as their own? ☐
- work on questions or problems which have enabled them to:
- AT6 – collect a variety of everyday materials? ☐
- AT6 – look for similarities and differences in everyday materials, such as cooking ingredients, water, chocolate and wax? ☐
- AT13 – explore and investigate ways of changing everyday materials by dissolving, squashing, pouring, twisting and bending? ☐
- AT13 – explore and investigate the effect of heating water, wax and chocolate? ☐
- AT13 – explore and investigate how hot or cold water and other materials are when they melt or solidify and relate this to temperature measured by a thermometer? ☐

Has the work pupils were engaged in allowed them to:

- AT1 • talk about the purposes of recording results? ☐
- AT1 • record results by drawing pictures, drawing block graphs and completing tables and bar charts? ☐
- AT1 • sort and group objects and events, such as: ☐
  - materials which melt in the sun or in heat and those which do not? ☐
  - substances which dissolve in water and those which do not? ☐
- AT1 • distinguish between a fair and an unfair test; for example, dissolving different amounts of jelly in the same amount of water? ☐
- AT1 • interpret findings by linking variables such as the amount of heat and whether chocolate will melt? ☐
- AT1 • describe activities carried out by sequencing the major features; for example, the steps taken in a baking activity? ☐
- AT1 • describe the best way of recording their activities? ☐
- AT1 • relate their findings to previous ideas and experiences? ☐
- AT1 • reflect upon how their procedures might be improved? ☐

Learning
Have the children demonstrated that they can:

Level 1
- AT6 • talk to you about the colour, texture and shape of everyday substances such as ice, water, wax and chocolate? ☐
- AT6 • tell you what happens when everyday substances are squashed, stretched or cooked? ☐
- AT1 • make observations of everyday substances, including cooking ingredients, and talk about their observations? ☐

Level 2
- AT6 • tell you about the similarities and differences in everyday materials? ☐
- AT6 • sort and group materials according to their characteristics? ☐
- AT6 • tell you what happens to materials when they are heated or cooled? ☐
- AT13 • tell you whether things feel 'hot' or 'cold' to their touch? ☐
- AT1 • identify simple variables such as hard/soft, hot/cold, rigid/bendy? ☐
- AT1 • ask questions and suggest ideas of the 'how' and 'why' variety? ☐
- AT1 • record findings in charts and drawings? ☐
- AT1 • list and collate observations? ☐
- AT1 • interpret findings by associating one factor with another, such as some substances melting at high temperatures and solidifying at low temperatures? ☐

Level 3
- AT6 • give some examples of those materials which occur naturally and those which are made from raw ingredients? ☐
- AT6 • list the similarities and differences in everyday substances, such as wax, ice, water and chocolate? ☐
- AT13 • tell you that they can measure how hot or cold things are by reading the temperature on a thermometer? ☐
- AT1 • formulate hypotheses? ☐
- AT1 • distinguish between a fair and an unfair test? ☐
- AT1 • record findings in tables and bar charts? ☐
- AT1 • describe activities carried out by sequencing the major features? ☐

Bishop Grosseteste College 1990. Copying permitted for purchasing schools only. This material is not 'copyright free'.

MATERIALS

UNIT 20
EVERYDAY MATERIALS: SAND, WOOD, METAL, PLASTICS, PAPER, CLAY, FABRICS (INCLUDING MAGNETS)

Opportunities for learning

The range of suggestions in this unit provides children with the following opportunities from the **programme of study** for key stage 1:

- to explore and investigate the properties of everyday, natural and manufactured materials and the effects of using simple processes on them
- to explore and investigate a variety of magnetic and non-magnetic materials
- to develop their investigative skills and understanding of science in the context of explorations and investigations

The suggestions for practical activities and discussion outlined in this unit provide children with the experiences necessary to facilitate attainment up to level 3.

Topics

Many topics provide children with opportunities for finding out about everyday materials: sand, wood, metal, plastics, paper, clay, fabrics (including magnets). Some examples are:

MY HOME	Properties of materials Sorting and grouping materials
OURSELVES	Properties of different fabrics
THE BUILDING SITE	Materials used by different trades Sorting and grouping materials for different criteria

The flow-diagram in section 1 (figure 3, pp. 4–5) will help you identify further topics.

Classroom materials

The following Nelson Science materials support this unit:

Picture Resource Book 3

- p. 15 – wood pulp
- p. 16 – high magnification of wool and nylon
- p. 17 – sheep-shearing

Planning and Preparation

- p.18 – cotton-picking
- p.19 – iron ore

Science Discussion Books for key stage 1
- finding out about materials

Science Explorers
- **Science Explorer, Carrying Out Surveys 1**
- **Science Explorer, Experimenting 1**
- **Science Explorer, Problem Solving 1**

Related units
Children may ask questions which will provide opportunities for finding out about the content of other units. For example:

- light, shadows, colours and mirrors – unit 1
- sounds – unit 2
- using materials to make structures – unit 21

Resources and equipment
- a range of pieces of wood, both hard and soft
- a range of objects made from metal
- a range of objects made from plastic
- a selection of different paper, such as tissue, sugar, waxed
- a variety of fabrics
- magnets
- a compass

In the Classroom

Getting started

Starting points
Work on everyday materials: sand, wood, metal, plastics, paper, clay, fabrics (including magnets) can arise from:

children talking about:
- their observations of different materials
- how and where different materials are used

children using their senses to:
- touch and manipulate materials

children making collections of:
- everyday materials
- objects made from different materials
- clothes made from different fabrics

children visiting:
- a building site

children playing in:
- the sand tray
- the water tray

Asking questions
The activities outlined above could lead to questions such as:

I wonder whether . . .
- any of the materials feel the same as any of the others?
- magnets push and pull each other?
- all magnets are the same strength?
- the magnet will attract objects through different materials?

What happens if . . .
- any of the materials is bent?
- any of the materials is scratched?
- any of the materials is twisted?
- any of the materials is stretched?
- any of the materials is put into water?
- any of the materials is dropped?
- water is poured onto any of the materials?
- any of the materials is put close to a magnet?

Can we find a way to . . .
- change the shape of any of the materials?
- change the colour of any of the materials?
- join two pieces of any of the materials together?
- make a magnetic toy?

Gathering information

Encourage children to think of ways of **gathering information** to help answer these questions.

Investigations which might follow these questions are outlined on pp. 173–176.

Ideas for taking these investigations further are given below.

Further investigations

Carrying out surveys
Collecting information about:
- the properties of everyday materials
- make comparisons between the kinds of material buildings are made from
- sort and group different fabrics that clothes are made from
- the use and effects of magnets
- find out how magnets are used
- collect pictures and everyday items which show magnets in use

Experimenting
- investigating ways in which magnets work through different materials
- construct toys which can be controlled using magnets; for example, a boat

Solving practical problems
- using materials to construct a strong bridge
- use materials which will not bend
- preserving materials from the weather
- use paint or varnish on a construction to be used outside

Handling information

Recording findings

Our magnets can pick up		Our magnets can't pick up	
⊙	the tin lid	⊸	the brass key
⊸	the steel key	◯	the gold ring
✂	the steel scissors	◯	the silver ring
⊢	the steel nail		

172

In the Classroom

Encourage the children to think about ways in which their findings can be recorded.

Talk with the children about your reasons for choosing a particular method of recording.

Findings from practical problem-solving activities can be recorded through drawing and writing.

> 5th october mark Scarbro
> Box
> On Friday we made a wall. we made the wall out of boxes. Then we sellotaped it together. It was stronger after we put the sellotape on it. But even with the sellotape it is still weak. If you build a wall with bricks it would stay up if you put cement with the bricks it would be a lot stronger.

Findings from surveys and experiments can be recorded individually or as a group by:

- using simple charts and pictograms
- using tables and bar charts

| The materials we collected when we visited the building site ||||
Material	Sticks to a magnet	Floats	Bends	Lets light through
Wood	✗	✓	✗	✗
Sugar paper	✗	✓	✓	✓
Plastic	✓	✗	✗	✗
Metal	✗	✓	✓	✗

Interpreting findings

Encourage children to link findings and observations, and thus try to establish and express cause-and-effect relationships.

Help children to link the 'weight' of objects with their ability to float, and the strength of any material with the amount of weight it will support.

Review points

The following are useful talking points:

Our investigations

- the questions we asked
- how we planned
- how we collected information
- how and why we recorded
- what we found out

Making connections

- the **origins of and differences between** natural materials, such as wood and wool, and manufactured materials, such as plastics and polyester
- people **who would use a compass**, such as walkers or pilots
- how a **compass** can help people with **directions**
- when we might need to **use a compass**

Safety

Ensure that the children:

- do not put magnets near a compass or a watch – although magnets are not dangerous they can affect other equipment
- do not inhale any glue substances

Investigations

I wonder whether...

- **any of the materials feels the same as any of the others?**

In the Classroom

The children can **use their senses** to find similarities and differences between any and all of the materials; for example, wood and metal.

Several objects made from different materials could be put into a 'feely' bag or box; for instance, a plastic and a metal comb, different types of paper, a soft toy and a wooden toy.

- **magnets push and pull each other?**

The children can **play** with magnets and describe how they feel.

They should **find out** what magnets can do to a variety of materials; for example, how they push, pull, raise and turn materials.

- **all magnets are the same strength?**

The children can **make a collection** of different types of bar and horseshoe magnet.

They could **investigate** things like which magnets pick up most paperclips, how long a train of paperclips the magnet will pull, etc.

- **the magnet will attract objects through different materials?**

The children can use a magnet to try to attract objects through paper, water or wood.

They could **predict** whether or not they can move magnetic materials by holding a magnet under a table, or behind a piece of paper.

What happens if . . .

- **any of the materials is bent.**

In the Classroom

- any of the materials is scratched?
- any of the materials is twisted?

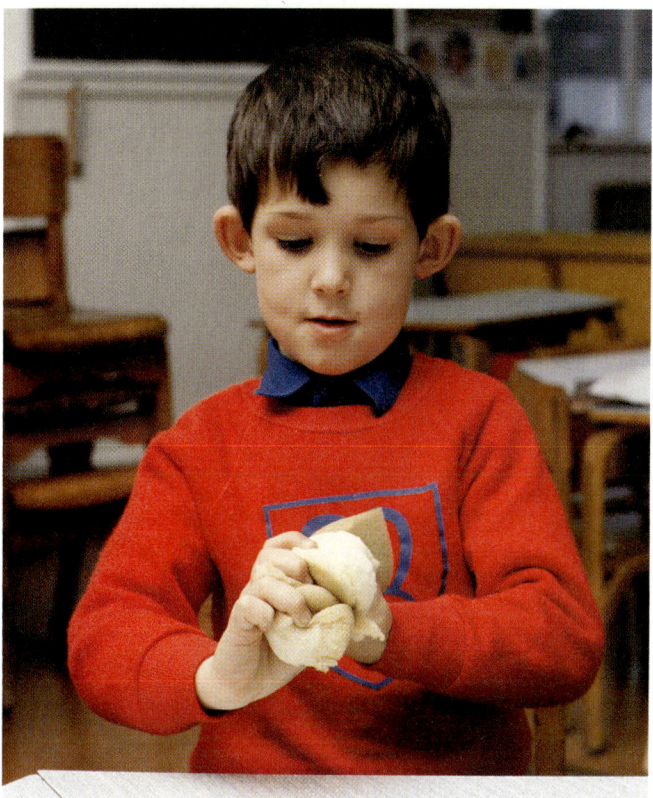

- any of the materials is stretched?
- any of the materials is put into water?

- any of the materials is dropped?
- water is poured onto any of the materials?
- any of the materials is put close to a magnet?

The children can **predict** what would happen and then manipulate any and all of the materials.

They could **gather information** about the properties of different materials.

They could begin to **sort and group** materials according to their properties; for example, materials which will stretch and materials which will not stretch: materials which sink and materials which float.

Can we find a way to . . .

- change the shape of any of the materials?

The children can **gather information** about how they can change the shape of materials, such as paper or fabric, by processes such as squashing, folding and bending.

They could begin to **identify** the characteristics in materials which enable them to be manipulated.

175

In the Classroom

- **change the colour of any of the materials?**

The children can add water to the material.

They could coat the material with wax or oil.

They could use natural or manufactured dyes to change the colour of the material, especially fabric.

- **join two pieces of any of the materials together?**

The children can use a number of adhesives or fasteners to join materials.

They could find out which materials sellotape, glue, or nails will hold together.

- **make a magnetic toy?**

The children can make a fishing game. They can cut the fish from card and attach a paperclip to the mouth of each fish. Rods can be made from thin dowelling, with magnets attached to the end of string which is wound round the rods.

Evaluation Checklist

Unit . . . .   Date . . . .

Teaching
Have the children been provided with opportunities to:

- work on questions or problems which they have accepted as their own? ☐
- work on questions or problems which have enabled them to:

AT6	– gather together a variety of different materials?	☐
AT6	– explore and investigate a variety of different materials to find similarities and differences?	☐
AT6	– explore and investigate ways of changing a variety of materials by using simple manipulative processes and treating surfaces?	☐
AT11	– explore and investigate a range of materials to see if they are attracted to magnets?	☐

Has the work pupils were engaged in allowed them to:

AT1	• talk about the purposes of recording results?	☐
AT1	• record results by drawing pictures and completing tables and bar charts?	☐
AT1	• sort and group objects, such as:	
	– materials which float and those that do not?	☐
	– materials which are attracted to a magnet and those which are not?	☐
	– materials which are hard and those which are not?	☐
AT1	• measure using non-standard and simple standard measuring skills; for example, how far different fabrics stretch, or how much weight materials will hold before they bend or tear?	☐
AT1	• distinguish between a fair and an unfair test?	☐
AT1	• interpret findings by linking variables?	☐
AT1	• describe activities carried out by sequencing the major features?	☐
AT1	• discuss their observations and ideas with other children?	☐
AT1	• describe the best way of recording their activities?	☐
AT1	• relate their findings to previous ideas and experiences?	☐
AT1	• reflect upon how their procedures might be improved?	☐

Learning
Have the children demonstrated that they can:

Level 1

AT6	• talk to you about the shape, colour and texture of a wide variety of objects made from different materials?	☐
AT6	• tell you what happens to a variety of different materials when they are manipulated or changed in some way?	☐
AT1	• make observations about a variety of different materials, objects and magnets and talk about their observations?	☐

Level 2

AT6	• tell you about the similarities and differences in materials both before and after they have been changed?	☐
AT6	• sort and group a wide variety of materials for a number of different criteria?	☐
AT11	• tell you which materials are attracted to a magnet and which materials are not?	☐
AT1	• identify simple variables such as hard/soft, rough/smooth, transparent/opaque?	☐
AT1	• ask questions and suggest ideas of the 'how' and 'why' variety?	☐
AT1	• measure using non-standard and standard units?	☐
AT1	• record findings in charts and drawings?	☐
AT1	• list and collate observations?	☐

Level 3

AT6	• tell you that materials such as wood occur naturally, but others such as plastic are made from raw materials?	☐
AT6	• make a list of the similarities and differences in a variety of everyday materials?	☐
AT1	• formulate hypotheses?	☐
AT1	• distinguish between a fair and an unfair test?	☐
AT1	• record findings in tables and bar charts?	☐
AT1	• describe activities carried out by sequencing the major features?	☐

Bishop Grosseteste College 1990. Copying permitted for purchasing schools only. This material is not 'copyright free'.

MATERIALS

UNIT 21
USING MATERIALS TO MAKE STRUCTURES

Opportunities for learning
The range of suggestions in this unit provides children with the following opportunities from the **programme of study** for key stage 1:
- to explore and investigate how everyday materials change when they are used in construction
- to explore and investigate the effects of forces on materials used in construction
- to develop their investigative skills and understanding of science in the context of explorations and investigations

The suggestions for practical activities and discussion outlined in this unit provide children with the experiences necessary to facilitate attainment up to level 3.

Topics
Many topics provide children with opportunities for finding out about using materials to make structures. Some examples are:

TOYS	Constructing a toy
BUILDINGS	Constructing strong shapes Constructing models Testing strength

The flow-diagram in section 1 (figure 3, pp.4–5) will help you identify further topics.

Classroom materials
The following Nelson Science materials support this unit:

Picture Resource Book 3
- p.10 – suspension bridges
- p.11 – arch bridges
- p.12 – pyramids
- p.13 – the Eiffel Tower
- p.14 – tall chimneys

Science Discussion Books for key stage 1
- finding out about materials

Science Explorers
- **Science Explorer, Problem Solving 1**

Related units
Children may ask questions which will provide opportunities for finding out about the content of other units. For example:
- how to make things move – unit 17

Planning and Preparation

- everyday materials: sand, wood, metal, plastics, paper, clay, fabrics (including magnets) – unit 20

Resources and equipment

- a selection of everyday waste materials such as card, paper, straws, lids, cereal packets, boxes and tubes.
- construction kits such as LEGO, DUPLO and MECCANO, and building blocks
- adhesives such as Marvin, Sellotape and Copydex
- metal fasteners and elastic bands

In the Classroom

Getting started

Starting points
Work on using materials to make structures can arise from:

children playing with:
- construction kits

children making:
- models from everyday materials

children visiting:
- an industrial museum
- a bridge
- a windmill
- a building site

children watching a television programme about:
- the construction of buildings or the variety of their shapes and sizes

Asking questions
The activities outlined above could lead to questions such as:

> **Can we find a way to . . .**
> - **build a tall tower?**
> - **build a bridge?**
> - **construct a boat with a sail?**
> - **construct a model of a building?**

Gathering information
Encourage children to think of ways of **gathering information** to help answer these questions.

Investigations which might follow these questions are outlined on pp. 181–182.

Ideas for taking these investigations further are given below.

Further investigations

> **Carrying out surveys**
> **Collecting information about:**
> - materials used in constructions
> – sort and group materials to find out which will make a strong bridge or tower without bending
> – find out the best shape for a boat or a sail on a boat
> – make comparisons between the materials used to build their homes or school

> **Experimenting**
> - investigating the strength of materials
> – treat the surfaces of materials such as card or paper to make them stronger
> – use wax, glue, paint or varnish to make paper more rigid

> **Solving practical problems**
> - measuring the force of wind
> – construct a wind sock or wind gauge
> – find out which materials make the best wind socks and/or rain gauges

Review points
The following are useful talking points:

Our investigations
- the questions we asked
- how we planned
- how we collected information
- how and why we recorded
- what we found out

Making connections
- the **different materials** which are used in the construction of buildings; for example, steel, concrete, glass and wood
- the importance to the strength of a structure not just of the strength of the material, but also of **how the structure is made**
- structures which have **existed a long time**, such as the pyramids, Stonehenge or other stone circles

Safety
Ensure that the children:
- are shown the correct techniques for using scissors and knives
- carefully handle glue – some glues are dangerous because of their inflammability and because of the risks of inhalation

Handling information

Recording findings
Encourage the children to think about ways in which their findings can be recorded.

Talk with the children about your reasons for choosing a particular method of recording.

Findings from practical problem-solving activities can be recorded through drawing and writing.

In the Classroom

Findings from surveys and experiments can be recorded individually or as a group by:
- using simple charts and pictograms
- using tables and bar charts

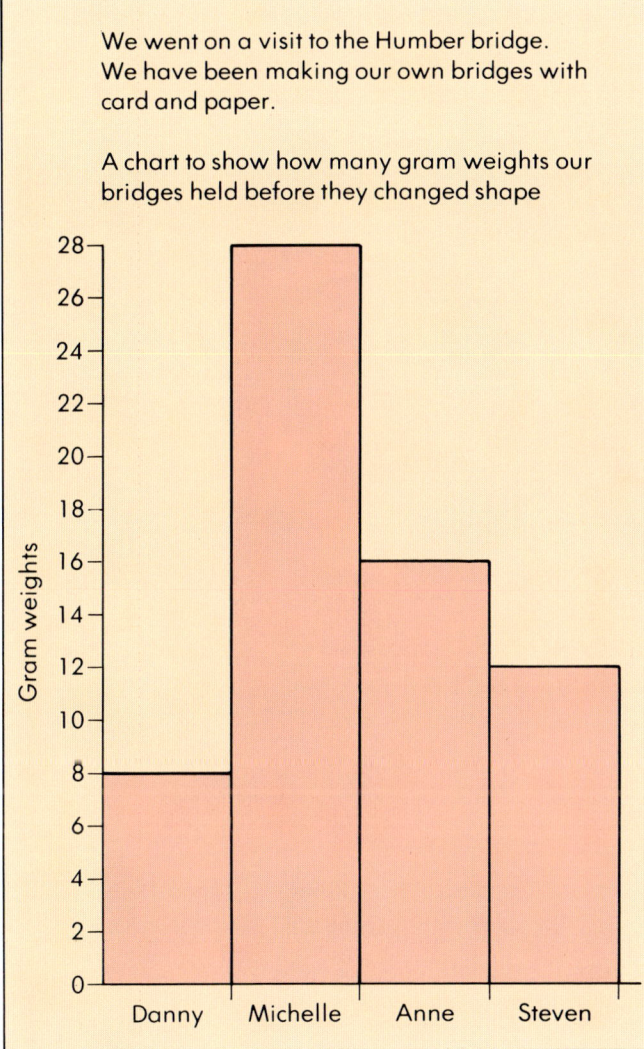

We went on a visit to the Humber bridge. We have been making our own bridges with card and paper.

A chart to show how many gram weights our bridges held before they changed shape

They could **use** building bricks or construction kits, or **design and make towers** using rolled newspaper, card or dowelling.

Interpreting findings

Encourage children to link findings and observations, and thus try to establish and express cause-and-effect relationships – for example, between the strength of a structure and the material used, and/or its shape; between the height and/or width of a tower and its stability.

Investigations

Can we find a way to...

- **build a tall tower?**

By constructing or building towers of different shapes, the children can begin to **investigate** which shapes make more stable structures.

They could then **devise tests** to see if their tall tower was strong or stable.

In the Classroom

- **build a bridge?**

The children can **design and make** bridges using paper, card or wood.

They could **test out** how strong their bridge is by putting weights on it.

They could **observe** how much weight the bridge will hold before the structure begins to change shape.

- **construct a boat with a sail?**

The children can **test out** which material makes a good sail for a boat.

They could **use** tissue paper, newspaper, and different types of fabric.

By using a hairdryer to simulate the wind, children could **find out** about the materials changing shape and which materials helps the boat to travel well.

- **construct a model**

The children can use everyday materials to **construct** a model relating to the theme or topic they are studying.

They could begin to **collect information** about the effects of treating the surface of materials, and also the effects of forces.

They could **find out** which materials will squash, which they can paint, which will stick together and which will bend.

Evaluation Checklist

Unit.......... Date..........

Teaching
Have the children been provided with opportunities to:

- work on questions or problems which they have accepted as their own? ☐
- work on questions or problems which have enabled them to:

AT6 – collect and talk about a variety of everyday materials? ☐

AT6 – look for similarities and differences in a variety of materials used in constructions? ☐

AT6 – work with and change a variety of materials used in constructions by using simple processes, such as bending, twisting and treating surfaces? ☐

AT10 – explore and talk about how to make things move, stop them moving and change the shape of things? ☐

Has the work pupils were engaged in allowed them to:

AT1 • talk about the purposes of recording results? ☐

AT1 • sort and group objects and events, such as:
– materials that start to bend when weights are put on them and those that do not? ☐

AT1 • measure using non-standard and simple standard measuring skills;
for example, how tall they can build a tower before it falls down? ☐

AT1 • distinguish between a fair and an unfair test? ☐
AT1 • interpret findings by linking variables? ☐
AT1 • describe activities carried out by sequencing the major features? ☐
AT1 • discuss their observations and ideas with other children? ☐
AT1 • describe the best way of making a record of their activities? ☐
AT1 • relate their findings to previous ideas and experiences? ☐
AT1 • reflect upon how their procedures might be improved? ☐

Learning
Have the children demonstrated that they can:

Level 1
AT6 • talk about the shape, colour and texture of the materials they are using in their structures? ☐

AT6 • tell you what happens to the materials they are using in their structures when they are squashed, are stretched or have had their surfaces treated? ☐

AT1 • make observations about the structures they are making and talk about their observations? ☐

Level 2
AT6 • tell you about the similarities and differences in their construction materials both before and after they have been changed? ☐

AT6 • sort and group a variety of materials for a number of different criteria? ☐

AT1 • ask questions and suggest ideas of the 'how' and 'why' variety? ☐

AT1 • measure using non-standard and standard units? ☐

AT1 • list and collate observations? ☐

Level 3
AT6 • tell you about some of the materials which occur naturally, such as wood, and some which are made from raw materials, such as plastic? ☐

AT6 • make a list of the similarities and differences in the materials used in their constructions? ☐

AT10 • tell you that their constructions will begin to change shape or move when forces are acting on them? ☐

AT1 • formulate hypotheses? ☐
AT1 • distinguish between a fair and an unfair test? ☐
AT1 • measure using simple measuring instruments, such as a ruler, to the nearest labelled division? ☐
AT1 • describe activities carried out by sequencing the major features? ☐

Bishop Grosseteste College 1990. Copying permitted for purchasing schools only. This material is not 'copyright free'.

Evaluation Checklist for IT

This checklist covers attainment target 12: scientific aspects of information technology (IT) including microelectronics.

Unit.......... Date..........

Teaching

Have the children been provided with opportunities to:

- use tape-recorders to record their work? ☐
- use television and video to extend their work in science? ☐
- use a computer for:
  - word processing? ☐
  - data handling? ☐

Has the work pupils were engaged in allowed them to:

- talk about the range of everyday devices which communicate information in the form of text, sound and images over long distances, such as:
  - television? ☐
  - radio? ☐
  - walkie-talkies? ☐
  - telephone? ☐
- talk about the range of everyday devices which can be used to store information, such as:
  - tape-recorder? ☐
  - answering machine? ☐
  - computer? ☐
  - video? ☐
  - calculator? ☐
  - digital watch? ☐
- retrieve and select text, number, sound or graphics stored on a computer, through:
  - word processing? ☐
  - data handling? ☐

Learning

Have the children demonstrated that they can:

Level 1

- talk about *some* of the everyday devices which receive text, sound and images over long distances? ☐
- talk about the *variety* of means of communicating information over long distances, such as television, radio, walkie-talkies, telephone? ☐

Level 2

- talk about the range of everyday devices which can store information, such as computer, tape-recorder, answering machine, video, digital watch, stopwatch, calculator? ☐

Level 3

- talk about the variety of ways in which information can be stored electronically? ☐
- store information-using devices such as tape recorders, digital watches and simple robotics? ☐
- retrieve and select text, number, sound or graphics stored on a computer through:
  - word processing? ☐
  - data handling? ☐

Bishop Grosseteste College 1990. Copying permitted for purchasing schools only. This material is not 'copyright free'.

Section 4
Science in Play Activities

For the sake of simplicity, science can be described as reality; it is the outside world with which the child has to come to terms. The inner world of feelings, fantasy and imagination forms an integral part of the dynamic process of accommodation or adaptation to the changing environment with which from birth onwards the senses are confronted. Science assumes that there is a reason for everything, and it is one of the functions of the educators to help the child to accommodate by using his intellectual powers to solve the problems of a changing reality with which he is continually faced. This can best be encouraged in the early years by providing the young child with suitable experiences, and presenting them alongside thought-provoking language.

Margaret Tait
International Journal of Early Childhood, 13 (1981) 2, pp. 158–162 'Fostering the growth of scientific attitudes in young children'.

This section is designed to help the teacher recognise and realise the potential for scientific learning experiences in a range of play provision.

Play activities are one of the major vehicles through which young children begin to acquire knowledge and understanding of science and the skills of scientific exploration. The following five play activities are explored here, with suggestions for exploiting their scientific learning potential:

- the sand tray
- the water tray
- toys
- role play
- modelling with everyday materials

The relationship between the activities and the National Curriculum attainment targets is spelled out in figure 16, so that the teacher is able to see how play activities contribute to learning in science.

Whilst we recognise that the essence of play is independent activity over extended periods of time, teacher intervention in the form of 'thought-provoking language' can help to mediate and extend children's learning.

Figure 16 Opportunities in each activity

Activity	Attainment targets for key stage 1													
	1	2	3	4	5	6	9	10	11	12	13	14	15	16
The sand tray	•			•		•	•	•						
The water tray	•	•				•		•			•	•	•	
Toys	•	•	•			•		•	•	•	•	•	•	
Role play	•	•	•	•	•	•	•	•		•	•		•	
Modelling with everyday materials	•	•				•	•	•			•	•	•	

Science in Play

For each of the five play activities we have provided:

- an initial list of general pointers for making the most of the activity as a resource for children's scientific learning. This shows the relationship between the activity and the knowledge and understanding attainment targets.
- specific guidance on a number of the general pointers, in this format:

Attainment target and related experiences **Dates . . .**	☐
Resources	☐☐
Suggestions for initiating activities	☐☐
Questions which stimulate activities	☐☐
Intervention to give the activity direction	☐☐

The specific guidance is provided only for a selection of the general pointers, as examples. It is not meant to be prescriptive: the teacher will have additional ideas for initiating and developing these play activities.

Teachers can use these photocopiable guidance sections as checklists for planning provision of resources, and for recording children's play experience over time.

Science in Play

The sand tray

AT	Opportunities
AT4 Genetics and evolution	Wet sand – comparison of sizes of hand prints and foot prints
AT6 Types and uses of materials	Differences between dry and wet sand Pattern making Pouring dry sand Sieves and holes Dry sand changing its form
AT9 Earth and atmosphere	Different types of soil and sand Collecting samples of different malleable materials Soil
AT10 Forces	Modelling and 'take shape' moulds Diggers, cars and lorries Wheels in sand, and how they move Sand toys

AT4 Foot and hand prints **Date(s) . . .**		☐
Resources	Wet sand Themselves Pets	☐ ☐ ☐
Suggestions and questions	Decide what to make patterns with Make hand or foot prints Compare and contrast the sizes and shapes Which is the biggest/smallest longest/shortest? Look at animals' prints and patterns	☐ ☐ ☐ ☐ ☐
Intervention	What does it feel like – soft, wet, cold, etc? Which is the biggest print? Talk about the difference between pet' prints and yours	☐ ☐ ☐

© Bishop Grosseteste College 1990. Copying permitted for purchasing school only. This material is not 'copyright free'.

Science in Play

AT6 Pouring/wet and dry sand Date(s)...		☐
Resources	Dry and/or wet sand	☐
	Various containers – sieve, scoop, spoon, funnel	☐
Suggestions and questions	How did you fill the container?	☐
	Can you find a way to make a pattern with sand?	☐
	What happens if sand is poured from nigh up?	☐
Interventions	Talk about wet/dry	☐
	Which is the best pourer?	☐

AT9 Differences and similarities in natural materials Date(s)...		☐
Resources	Dry sand and soil	☐
	Hands	☐
	Trays	☐
	Containers of water	☐
Suggestions and questions	Describe the texture, touch, smell, feel and colour	☐
	Pour water onto the sand and soil	☐
Intervention	Talk about differences and similarities	☐
	Which is the lightest/darkest?	☐
	Which do you like best?	☐
	Why?	☐
	What have you noticed about wet sand and wet soil?	☐

© Bishop Grosseteste College 1990. Copying permitted for purchasing school only. This material is not 'copyright free'.

Science in Play

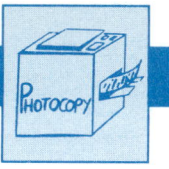

AT10 Modelling with moulds Date(s)...		☐
Resources	Dry sand Numerous moulds, buckets, spades, scoops Water (later)	☐ ☐ ☐
Suggestions and questions	How can you fill the mould? Can you build a castle? What happened when the water was added?	☐ ☐ ☐
Intervention	Which is best, dry or wet sand?	☐

AT10 Pushing and pulling in sand Date(s)...		☐
Resources	Two trays of sand – one wet, one dry Toy cars	☐ ☐
Suggestions and questions	What happened in dry sand? What happened in wet sand?	☐ ☐
Intervention	Which was fastest/slowest? Which is best? Which sand is best for the cars to move through? Why is that sand the best?	☐ ☐ ☐ ☐

© Bishop Grosseteste College 1990. Copying permitted for purchasing school only. This material is not 'copyright free'.

Science in Play

The water tray

AT	Opportunities
AT2 Variety of life	Bathing babies Washing dolls and dolls' clothes
AT6 Types and uses of materials	Sponges Bubbles Pouring from different containers
AT10 Forces	Shape containers Water wheels Corks Boats Wind-up water toys Different shaped materials
AT13 Energy	Ice Snow Warm water Wind-up toys
AT14 Sound and music	Sounds Dropping pebbles Squeezy bottles Blowing bubbles
AT15 Using light	Colour Reflections Sun on moving water Coloured water Sunlight sparkling, ripples etc.

© Bishop Grosseteste College 1990. Copying permitted for purchasing school only. This material is not 'copyright free'.

Science in Play

AT2 Bathing babies Date(s)...		☐
Resources	Bath	☐
	Soap	☐
	Cotton wool	☐
	Doll	☐
	Flannel/sponge	☐
	Powder tin	☐
	Hair brush	☐
Suggestions and questions	How should you hold the baby?	☐
	Do you need hot or cold water?	☐
	What does the soap do?	☐
	Why do you need soap?	☐
Intervention	Is your baby clean now?	☐
	Did you dry it?	☐
	What happens if the soap gets in its eye?	☐
	Where has the soap gone?	☐

AT6 Bubbles Date(s)...		☐
Resources	Washing-up liquid	☐
	Tubes	☐
	Straws	☐
	Sponges	☐
	Bubble pipes	☐
Suggestions and questions	Don't suck, you must blow!	☐
	What happens when you squeeze the sponge?	☐
Intervention	What makes the bubbles?	☐
	Which makes the biggest bubble?	☐
	What has happened to the water?	☐

© Bishop Grosseteste College 1990. Copying permitted for purchasing school only. This material is not 'copyright free'.

Science in Play

AT13 Snow Date(s)...		☐
Resources	Snow in water tray Indoors	☐ ☐
Suggestions and questions	Is it hot or cold? What does it feel like? What can you do with the snow? What's happening to it? What happens when you squeeze it?	☐ ☐ ☐ ☐ ☐
Intervention	Where has the snow gone? What made it happen? Where has the water come from?	☐ ☐ ☐

AT14 Sounds Date(s)...		☐
Resources	Water in tray Pebbles Squeezy bottles Action toys	☐ ☐ ☐ ☐
Suggestions and questions	Drop something into the water What happened? Does it make a noise?	☐ ☐ ☐
Intervention	Which makes the loudest noise? Which makes the biggest splash?	☐ ☐

© Bishop Grosseteste College 1990. Copying permitted for purchasing school only. This material is not 'copyright free'.

Science in Play

AT15 Reflection/light **Date(s) . . .**		☐
Resources	Sunshine (or torch) Water tray outside Jugs Funnels Watering cans Washing-up liquid bottles	☐ ☐ ☐ ☐ ☐ ☐
Suggestions and questions	Spray the water from high up What can you see?	☐ ☐
Intervention	What happens if you move the tray/spray the water/ splash the water? What makes the reflection ripple? What makes the water sparkle?	☐ ☐ ☐

© Bishop Grosseteste College 1990. Copying permitted for purchasing school only. This material is not 'copyright free'.

Science in Play

Toys

AT	Opportunities
AT2 Variety of life	Farm and zoo animals
AT3 Processes of life	Dolls
AT6 Types and use of materials	Construction toys – nuts, bolts, straws Water toys Kites Windmills
AT10 Forces	Physical outdoor construction Road safety toys – road layout Bikes, trucks, garages, ramp, slides, balls, rolling marbles Balloon - propelled models Elastic-band - propelled models Clockwork toys Cogs and cog-wheels
AT11 Electricity and magnetism	Magnetic trains – Brio Joining with magnetic toys
AT12 Information technology	Old clocks, radios and telephones
AT13 Energy	Clockwork toys Water wheels Wind-up toys
AT14 Sound and music	Making instruments Music boxes Jack-in-the-boxes
AT15 Using light	Torches

© Bishop Grosseteste College 1990. Copying permitted for purchasing school only. This material is not 'copyright free'.

Science in Play

AT2 Toy animals—care of living things Date(s) . . .		☐
Resources	Animals ☐ Building or geometric shapes/blocks ☐ Ground sheet ☐ Fencing ☐ Play people ☐ Models of farm tools ☐	
Suggestions and questions	What home will you make for this animal? ☐ What does it need to eat? ☐ Does it need to be near trees/rocks/pond/grass? ☐ Does it play? How does it play? ☐ What does it do? ☐ Who cares for it? ☐	
Intervention	Talk to children about what they have done and discuss particular animals' needs ☐	

AT6 Constructor straws – bending Date(s) . . .		☐
Resources	Constructor straws ☐	
Suggestions and questions	Can you make a flower? ☐ How many straws do you need to make your flower? ☐ Can you make a wheel? ☐	
Intervention	What else will bend? ☐ Why do the straws bend? ☐ How far do they bend? ☐ What else can you make? ☐	

© Bishop Grosseteste College 1990. Copying permitted for purchasing school only. This material is not 'copyright free'.

Science in Play

AT10 Making things move – cog-wheels Date(s)...		☐
Resources	Cog-wheels (interlocking)	☐
Suggestions and questions	Can you make the big/little/all the cogs move? ☐ How many wheels can you move by only turning one? ☐	
Intervention	Why do they move? ☐ What patterns did they make when they moved? ☐	

AT11 Experience of magnets Date(s)...		☐
Resources	Variety of magnets – different sizes and shapes ☐ Paperclips ☐ Coins ☐ Keys ☐ Feathers ☐ Shells ☐ Cork ☐ Nails ☐	
Suggestions and questions	What will the magnet pick up? ☐ Which magnet holds the most? ☐ Can you build with the magnet? ☐	
Intervention	Can the magnet make things move? ☐ Can you think of anything else the magnet will pick up or stick to? ☐	

© Bishop Grosseteste College 1990. Copying permitted for purchasing school only. This material is not 'copyright free'.

Science in Play

Role Play

AT	Opportunities
AT2 Variety of life	Family pets Rhymes and jingles – acting out Vet's corner – needs and welfare of animals Farms
AT3 Processes of life	Health centre – role of drugs Kitchen – feeding Home corner – setting the table Dentist Domestic play – child care – drama after story Hospital corner or clinic Café
AT4 Genetics and evolution	Dressing up – sizes: too big or too small Hairdressers Family life Domestic play – animals – drama after stories
AT5 Human influences on the earth	Dustbin men Cleaners, clearing up Collecting, gardening
AT6 Types and uses of materials	Shops Restaurant Chip shop Wood-working
AT9 Earth and atmosphere	Washing play Washing on line
AT10 Forces	Small imaginative toys, such as garage, dolls' house Police
AT12 Information technology	Radio, telephone etc. in home corner

© Bishop Grosseteste College 1990. Copying permitted for purchasing school only. This material is not 'copyright free'.

Science in Play

AT13 Energy	Café – food Home corner Garage Shop Dentist Cooking pretend food Dressing up
AT15 Using light	Shadow puppets

AT2 Vet's corner ☐
Date(s) . . .

Resources	Pictures and charts of animals ☐ Toy animals ☐ Stethoscope ☐ Bandages ☐ Cage, bowl, hutch etc. ☐
Suggestions and questions	Which animals might have injuries to their wings? ☐ Which animals might bite or scratch the vet? ☐
Intervention	How can you keep a rabbit/dog/cat etc. healthy? ☐ What food do these animals need? ☐ Which animals would you see in a vet's surgery? ☐

© Bishop Grosseteste College 1990. Copying permitted for purchasing school only. This material is not 'copyright free'.

Science in Play

AT3 Home corner Date(s)...		☐
Resources	Usual utensils Dolls TV Duster/hoover	☐ ☐ ☐ ☐
Suggestions and questions	What does your baby eat? What do Mum and Dad eat? Which shoes/clothes belong to whom? Why shouldn't you touch the iron etc?	☐ ☐ ☐ ☐
Intervention	Talk about the child's role Talk about safe play Why did you give your baby milk?	☐ ☐ ☐

AT4 Dressing up Date(s)...		☐
Resources	Variety of different sized clothes from a range of cultures Mirrors, pictures	☐ ☐
Suggestions and questions	What colour are your eyes? How many children have blue eyes? How are your clothes the same/different?	☐ ☐ ☐
Intervention	Why are there different eye colours? Talk about difference between clothes Why do girls' and boys' clothes differ?	☐ ☐ ☐

© Bishop Grosseteste College 1990. Copying permitted for purchasing school only. This material is not 'copyright free'.

Science in Play

AT13 Dentists Date(s) . . . ☐		
Resources	Usual utensils	☐
	Dentist chair	☐
	Toothbrushes/with paste	☐
	Teeth model/disclosing tablets	☐
	Foods (good and bad)	☐
Suggestions and questions	Why do you go to the dentist?	☐
	Who cleans their teeth and why?	☐
	Which foods are good/bad?	☐
	What happens if you don't clean your teeth?	☐
	Are your teeth sensitive?	☐
Intervention	Talk about being a dentist	☐
	Talk about being kind and careful	☐
	Talk about what it feels like to be in the dentist's chair	☐

AT15 Shadow puppets Date(s) . . . ☐		
Resources	Theatre	☐
	Puppets of different varieties	☐
Suggestions and questions	Can you make your shadow bigger/sharper?	☐
	Can you change the shape?	☐
	How many different shapes can you make?	☐
Intervention	What will happen if you use a black wall?	☐
	What did you do to make your shadow bigger?	☐
	What did you do to change the shape?	☐

© Bishop Grosseteste College 1990. Copying permitted for purchasing school only. This material is not 'copyright free'.

Science in Play

Modelling with everyday materials

AT	Opportunities
AT2 Variety of life	Modelling animals and plants Printing Sewing cloth, materials
AT6 Types and uses of materials	Cooking Natural material – clay, dough Collage Sawdust modelling Clay – soft/hard
AT9 Earth and atmosphere	Collecting samples of soil, sand, clay – use in/on models
AT10 Forces	Moulds Junk models Junk models wheeled Push – pull constructions
AT13 Energy	Cooking Modelling pretend food
AT14 Sound and music	Making musical instruments from junk materials
AT15 Using light	Model telescope Model binoculars

© Bishop Grosseteste College 1990. Copying permitted for purchasing school only. This material is not 'copyright free'.

Science in Play

AT2 Making models of a frog's life cycle ☐		
Date(s) . . .		
Resources	Clay	☐
	Tools – cutting tools, sponges, protection for work-surfaces	☐
	Tank of tadpoles	☐
	Books	☐
Suggestions and questions	Can you make the eggs?	☐
	What happens first?	☐
	What happens next?	☐
Intervention	Discuss the finished model	☐
	How many legs does the frog have at each stage?	☐

AT6 Baking bread ☐		
Date(s) . . .		
Resources	Flour yeast	☐
	Milk	☐
	Sugar	☐
	Utensils – sieves, measuring jug, spoons, knives, baking tins etc.	☐
Suggestions and questions	Why do we sieve the flour?	☐
	Where does the water go?	☐
	What does it smell like?	☐
	What do we add to make it less sticky?	☐
Intervention	Rising – what's happened to the size?	☐
	Cooking – is it still soft?	☐
	What's happened to the colour?	☐
	Has the smell changed?	☐
	What does it taste like?	☐
	Do you like it?	☐

© Bishop Grosseteste College 1990. Copying permitted for purchasing school only. This material is not 'copyright free'.

Science in Play

AT10 Moving transport – junk modelling Date(s) . . .		☐
Resources	Cheese boxes Straws Boxes Picture books	☐ ☐ ☐ ☐
Suggestions and questions	How many wheels has it got? What shape should they be? Is it a car or a lorry? How big is it? How many doors/windows?	☐ ☐ ☐ ☐ ☐
Intervention	How did you get the wheels to turn? Where does the driver sit? Why did you make it that size? Why won't it move?	☐ ☐ ☐ ☐

AT13 Modelling pretend food with dough **Food** Date(s) . . .		☐
Resources	Real fruit, to compare Dough mixture, paints and varnish	☐ ☐
Suggestions and questions	Have you chosen the real colour? Is your fruit the same size as the real one?	☐ ☐
Intervention	Do they feel the same? Can you eat them both? Do the real ones smell? Do they taste? Do they smell the same?	☐ ☐ ☐ ☐ ☐

© Bishop Grosseteste College 1990. Copying permitted for purchasing school only. This material is not 'copyright free'.